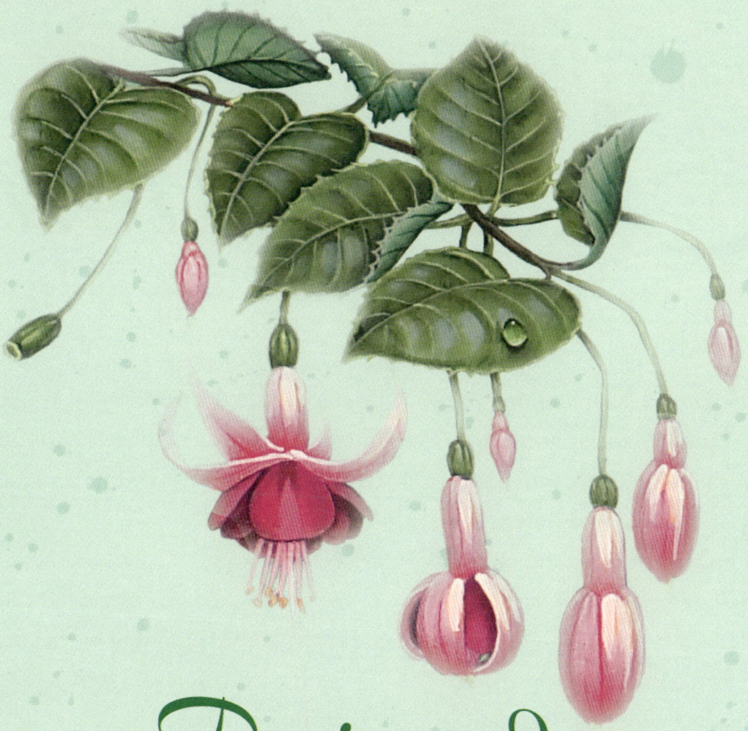

Painted Botanicals

By Barbara Baatz Hillman

Botanical drawings and paintings have been around for centuries in various mediums on old parchment, porcelain, wood, and many other surfaces. They add a wonderful old-world charm to a table or wall. I have tried to recreate the look of old botanicals in this book of projects for you to paint. There are four depictions of flowers and four of fruit, and a butterfly in each project adds color and beauty, just as they do in our gardens.

I hope this book provides you with many happy hours of painting, and some beautiful accessories for your home or for gifts.

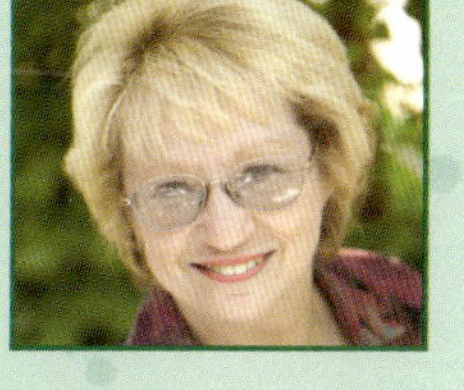

Contents

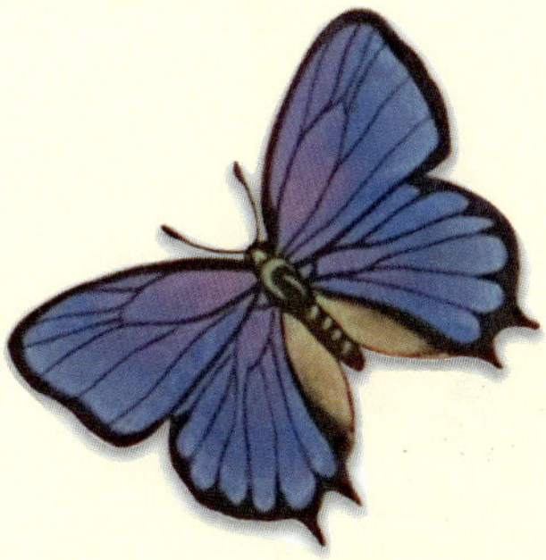

General Instructions

WOOD PREPARATION

1. Fill any holes in the wood with wood filler and allow to dry. Sand the wood with fine sandpaper, following the direction of the grain, until very smooth to the touch. Remove any dust from the surface by carefully wiping with a damp cloth.

2. If the project requires stain, seal the surface after applying the stain by spraying with a coat of *Delta Matte* or *Satin Interior Spray Varnish* or a water-based matte or satin varnish of your choice. This makes it easier to wipe off any paint that may get on the stained surface by mistake or while shading. It's also a good idea to spray a light coat over areas basecoated with black or other very dark colors, as they sometimes smear when the area is sanded or wiped off.

3. When you've finished painting your project and are happy with the way it looks, let it dry thoroughly. Erase any graphite lines that may have been overlooked and wipe the project with a damp cloth to remove any dust particles. Spray with several coats of water-based satin varnish. Let each coat dry completely before applying another.

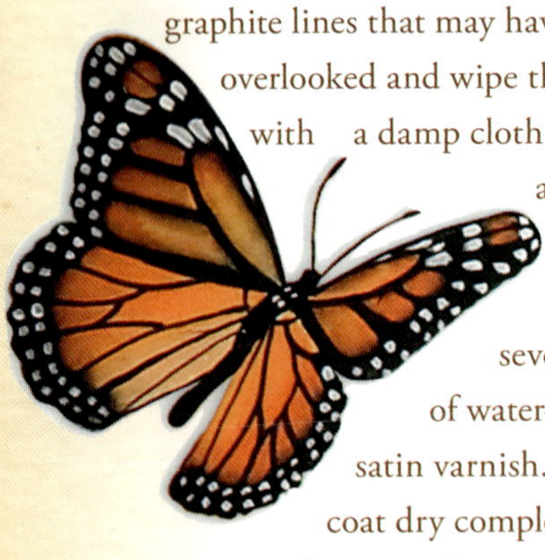

METAL PREPARATION

1. A metal surface needs to be completely clean and dry and free from any grease or oil. Depending on the shape and size, you may be able to put it in the dishwasher; otherwise, wash it thoroughly with detergent and dry on low heat in the oven.

2. When completely dry, coat the surface with *Delta Metal Primer*, following the instructions on the bottle. When this is dry, basecoat the metal. Paint on the prepared metal surface exactly the same way you would paint on a wood surface.

If the metal surface is pre-primed, such as the "Orange Tray" on page 32, no further preparation is necessary.

TRANSFERRING THE DESIGN

1. Trace the pattern onto tracing paper with a fine-point pen. Position the tracing paper over the prepared surface and tape one side down with transparent tape. Slip a piece of transfer paper (light or dark, depending on which shows up best) under the tracing paper and transfer only the basic outlines to the surface, using the small end of the stylus. Transfer details as needed. Use a light touch when transferring to avoid leaving indentations and to keep the graphite lines light. When transferring details onto a basecoated surface, make sure that the paint is completely dry or the graphite will transfer on much too heavily. You can use a hair dryer to speed the drying time if you'd like, but use it on the "warm" setting rather than "hot."

2. After transferring the lines to the painted surface, go over them lightly with a kneaded eraser so they can barely be seen. Once the painting on an area is finished and dry, completely erase any remaining lines with a white art eraser.

PAINTING

1. The colors used in a particular project are listed at the beginning of that project. Check the list before you start so everything is handy.

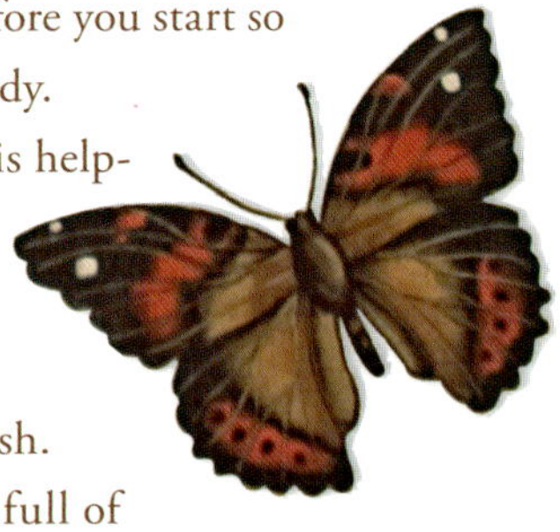

2. A wet palette is helpful for keeping the paint moist and for ease in loading your brush. Keep the sponge full of water and cover with the lid when you're not painting, and the paint will stay moist for days. Empty foam egg cartons are also handy. You can put paint in the egg indentations and sideload your brush for shading, using the inside of the flat top.

3. Keep two containers of water handy when painting: a *Loew-Cornell Brush Tub* with ribs on the bottom for easy brush cleaning, and a smaller one for dipping into with a clean brush for floating colors. Adding a couple of drops of *Delta Ceramcoat Color Float* to the smaller jar of water helps color float more evenly.

4. Always thin your paint sufficiently enough to smoothly cover an area. It's better to paint several thin coats than one thick coat that leaves ridges. The finished results will be well worth the extra effort. Instead of water, try adding a flow medium, such as *Jo Sonja's Flow*

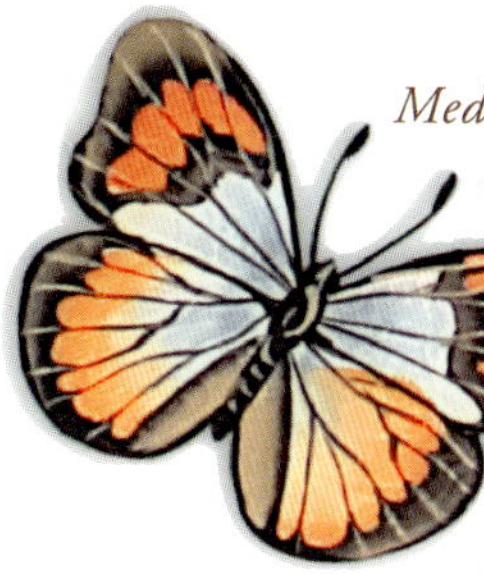

Medium to increase the fluidity of the paint so that it goes on more smoothly. However, if uneven build-up does occur, lightly sand the paint smooth with the sanding sponge or steel wool and wipe away any paint dust with a damp cloth. If just a light sanding is needed, rubbing with an unprinted brown paper bag works great.

5. When painting with red, yellow, orange, and some of the purples, it's helpful to use an undercoat of White or Light Ivory, since these colors are generally transparent and need quite a few coats for adequate coverage. The colors will also be truer and brighter if painted over a light basecoat.

6. When painting any project, always paint from back to front (i.e., background before foreground, leaves and stems before flowers or fruit, back petals before front petals).

SHADING

1. Add shading by floating color with a sideloaded brush. Choose the largest flat or angular brush that will comfortably fit the area to be shaded. (I prefer angular brushes for this, because they are easier to fit into tight little spaces.) Wet the brush and blot slightly on a paper towel—it should be moist but not wet. Dip about ¼" of the side of the brush into the paint, then stroke the brush on the wet palette several times until the paint is blended partway across the width of the brush. The other side of the brush should have clean water with no paint.

2. Lightly dampen the surface of the area to be shaded. This helps to get a smoother shading. Start with the lightest shading first. This is also the largest shaded area. You can go over the shading as many times as necessary to get a smooth, even shade, as long as you let the paint dry thoroughly between each application. If you go over the shading before it's dry, you'll lift the paint from the previous shading. Dampen the area again each time you add shading. The second shading (using a darker color) covers a much smaller area, and a still smaller area for any third shading.

GLAZING

Brushing a transparent color (glaze) over the base color adds more color and depth to an area than can be achieved with the base color alone. When glazing, if the color isn't already transparent, mix with a medium such as *Delta Gel Stain Medium* to make them more transparent. If this is necessary, it will be specified in the project instructions. If a medium is not specified, glaze by mixing the color with a small amount of water and brushing over the base color. Repeat when dry to deepen the color to your satisfaction.

USING RETARDER AND ANTIQUING MEDIUM

This medium is helpful for many different paint applications. I use it in this book for antiquing and for blending highlights. The main thing to remember is the medium must remain wet while you are blending or antiquing. If it starts to dry while you are working with it, stop, dry the surface thoroughly with your hair dryer, reapply the retarder, and continue.

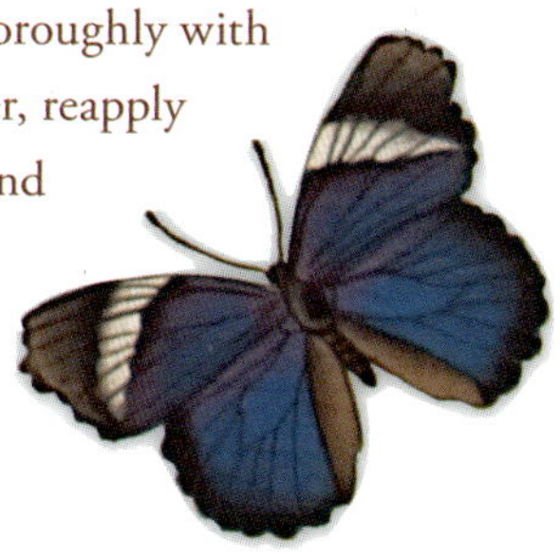

GENERAL SUPPLIES

Delta Ceramcoat Acrylic Paints
Delta Color Float
Delta Gel Blending Medium
Delta Matte or Satin Interior Spray Varnish or water-based equivalent
Delta Metal Primer
Delta Gel Stain Medium
Jo Sonja's Flow Medium
Jo Sonja's Retarder and Antiquing Medium
Loew-Cornell Brushes
Loew-Cornell Brush Tub and other small water containers
Masterson's Sta-Wet Palette
3M Superfine Sanding Sponge or steel wool
Black permanent ink fine-line pen
Brown paper bag
Double-ended stylus
Egg carton
Fine sandpaper
Hair dryer
Kneaded and white art erasers
Paper towels
Pencil
Soft cloth
Tracing paper
Transfer paper (dark and light)
Transparent ruler
Transparent tape
Wood filler

PROJECT SPECIFIC

Delta Antiquing Medium, Black
Delta Fine Crackle Finish, Steps 1 and 2
Langnickel Stylus Tool Set #RD90
Magic Sponge
All-purpose glue
Decorative hangers
Old toothbrush

RESOURCES

Refer to page 21

Cyclamen Box

Delicate cyclamen blossoms in a painted wicker basket bring garden color to your tabletop.

MATERIALS

PALETTE

Delta Ceramcoat Acrylics

Apple Green
Black
Blueberry
Blue Heaven
Blue Jay
Burnt Umber
Calypso Orange
Copen Blue
Dark Foliage Green
GP Purple
Light Foliage Green
Maple Sugar Tan
Medium Foliage Green
Peony
Pink Quartz
Pumpkin
Raspberry
Red Iron Oxide
Spice Brown
Spice Tan
Sweetheart Blush
Terra Cotta
Village Green
White
Yellow

BRUSHES

Loew-Cornell, Inc.

1" wash: Series 7550
#0 and #1 liners: Series 7350
#4, #8 and #10 shaders: Series 7300
¼", ½" and ⅜" angular shaders: Series 7400
#4 and #6 filberts: Series 7500

SURFACE

Large oval box, 9½" x 7" x 4" (item #WD1124-L, *Hofcraft*)
See Resources on page 21

OTHER SUPPLIES

Delta Gel Stain Medium
Print paper (optional)

PATTERN

Refer to pattern on page 19.

PREPARATION

Please read carefully the "General Instructions" in the front of the book before starting this project.

1. Fill any small holes around the top and bottom of the box and lid with wood filler and sand smooth.

2. Basecoat the sides of the box and lid with Spice Brown.

3. Starting at the overlap on the side of the box, mark ¼" from the edge, then mark off ½" increments around the box, top and bottom. Use these marks to paint thin vertical lines ½" apart all around the sides of the box with Spice Tan (see worksheet on page 7).

4. With a #4 shader and Spice Tan, start halfway between two of the vertical lines and paint a "wicker" stripe, slightly curved, across the vertical line and halfway to the next. Paint more stripes below the first, staying approximately the width of the brush apart, until reaching the bottom of the box. Paint the following vertical rows the same way, starting the top stripe between the two top stripes in the previous row. Continue around the box until it's covered. You'll need at least two coats of paint for good coverage.

5. Shade both sides of the wicker stripes with Burnt Umber.

6. Highlight the middle of each stripe with Maple Sugar Tan.

7. Paint a strip about ⅛" wide around the top and bottom of the box with Spice Tan, then float on a thin Burnt Umber shadow between these strips and the wicker. Paint the lip of the box with Spice Tan.

8. Place the lid on the box and mark off a vertical line, matching the placement to a vertical line on the box side, then paint the vertical lines and wicker the same as on the box sides. Remember to paint under the lip.

TOP

1. Transfer the oval line to the top and basecoat inside the oval with Copen Blue.

2. Shade around the edges of the Copen Blue with Blueberry, then spatter with Blueberry, using an old toothbrush.

3. Paint the edge around the oval with Spice Brown, then paint "wicker" stripes radiating out to the sides of the top using the #4 shader (see photo). Shade around the top and bottom of the wicker stripes with Burnt Umber (wipe off any that gets on the side of the lid), then highlight the middle of the stripes with Maple Sugar Tan.

4. Transfer the basic design to the top.

STEMS AND SEPALS

1. Basecoat the stems and sepals with Spice Tan.

2. Shade down both sides of the stems and sepals, where they come out of a flower or from behind another stem or a leaf, with Red Iron Oxide.

3. Deepen the shading with Burnt Umber. Paint a very fine line down each side of the stem, also with Burnt Umber.

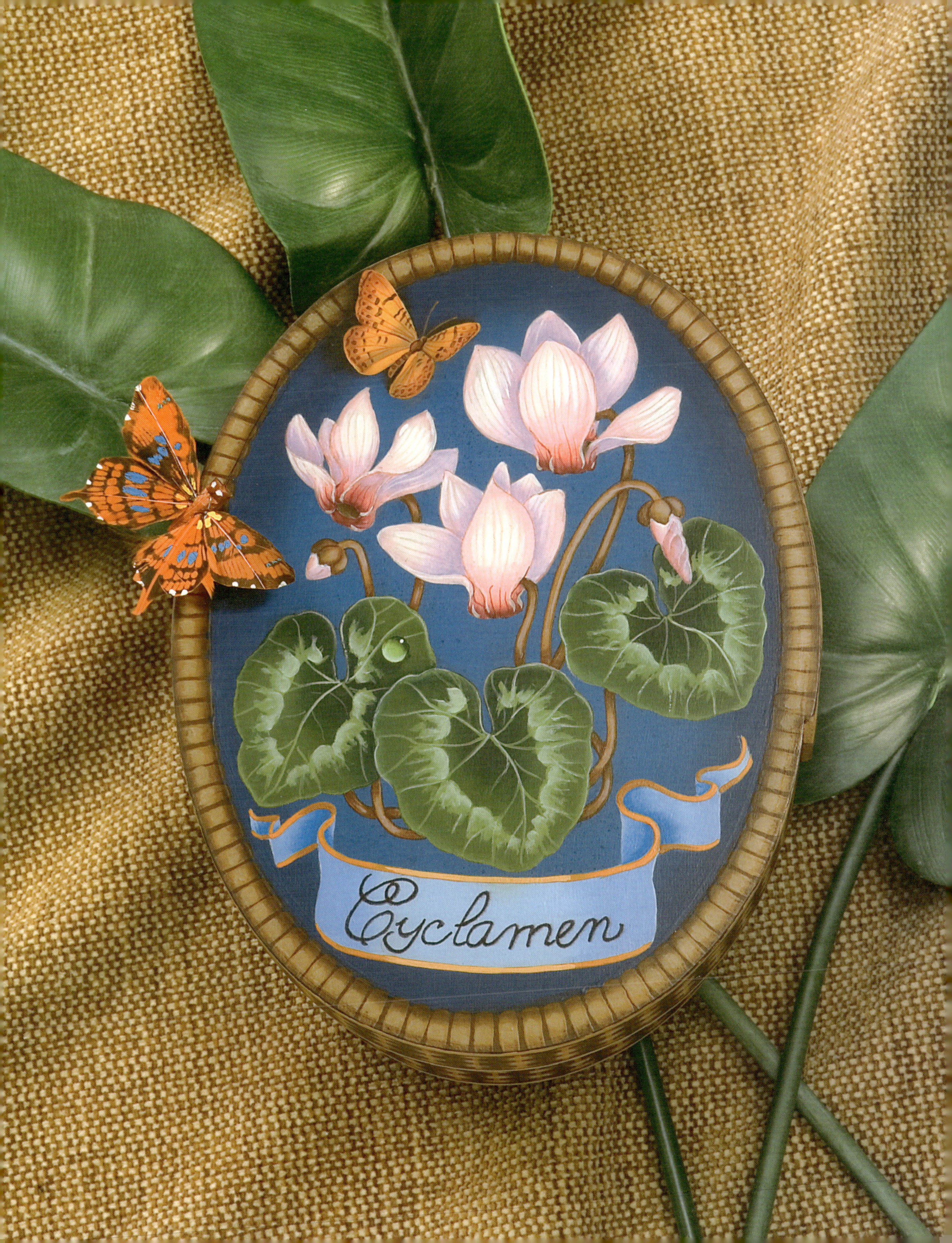
Cyclamen

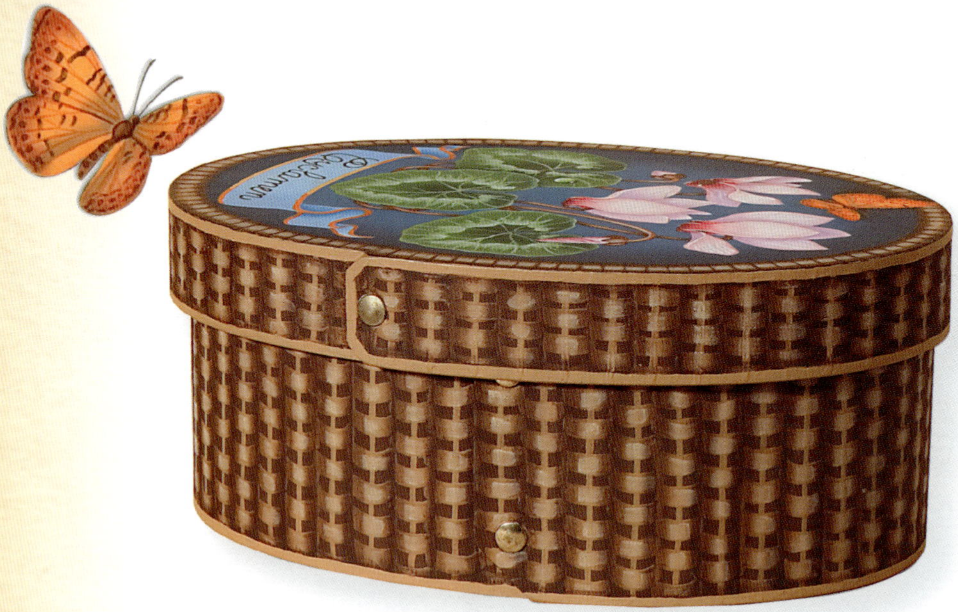

4. Highlight the stems and sepals with Pink Quartz.

LEAVES

1. Basecoat with Medium Foliage Green. Shade around the top edges and top center of each leaf with Dark Foliage Green. Shade the left leaf where it is overlapped by the middle leaf.
2. Highlight around the edges with Light Foliage Green, then dab on Light Foliage Green spots. Pull wiggly lines to one side, starting just above the center top of the leaf and following the curve of the leaf (refer to photo and worksheet).
3. Paint the veins with Light Foliage Green. With Village Green, highlight the spots and areas of the veins where needed.

WATER DROP

1. Shade around the bottom and partway up the left side of the drop shape with Dark Foliage Green. Paint the drop with Apple Green.
2. Shade the drop at the top right with Medium Foliage Green, then deepen at the top with Dark Foliage Green.
3. Highlight around the left and bottom with White, then add a White highlight dot to the top.

BLOSSOMS

1. Where the center of the flower is showing, paint with Spice Brown, then shade with Burnt Umber. Basecoat the petals with Peony. Shade around the edges with Pink Quartz, heavier around the base, then paint fine lines through each petal from the base to the tip, following the contour of the petal.
2. Deepen the shading at the base of the petals with Raspberry. Paint a fine, light line around each petal and overlap with Raspberry.
3. With a mix of Gel Stain Medium + GP Purple (1:1), shade between the petals and wherever they overlap.
4. At the base of each petal, add a shading of Sweetheart Blush, then paint a few thin lines going from the base about ¼" into the petal.
5. Highlight with White between the thin Pink Quartz lines in each petal, around the overlaps, and at the sides of the petals at the base.

BUDS

1. Basecoat the buds with Peony; shade along both sides and under the "folds" with Pink Quartz.
2. Deepen the shading around the left side and below the folds with Raspberry.
3. Glaze on the right side with a mix of GP Purple + Gel Stain Medium, then highlight with White.

BUTTERFLY

1. Basecoat the wings with Calypso Orange, then glaze with a thin coat of Yellow.
2. Shade around the edges of the wings with Pumpkin. Deepen around the outside edges with Terra Cotta. Shade the upper wings, close to the body and over the Pumpkin shading, with Spice Tan. Repeat the same on the lower wings, shading just above the lowest section.
3. Paint the body, antennae, and the veins in the wings with Terra Cotta.
4. Paint the details on the wings and body with Burnt Umber.

BANNER

1. Basecoat the banner with Blue Heaven. Shade around the overlapped areas and about ½" in on both sides of the center section with Blue Jay.
2. Deepen the shading around the overlapped areas with Copen Blue.
3. Paint a narrow strip around the top and bottom edges of the banner with Pumpkin. Paint over this in the darkest areas of the banner with Terra Cotta and in the lightest areas with Calypso Orange.
4. Write in the "Cyclamen" lettering with the black permanent ink fine-line pen.

FINISHING

1. Erase any remaining transfer lines. Clean off any paint from the brass buttons on the sides of the box and lid, then spray with a couple of coats of satin varnish.
2. Paint the inside of the box with a color of your choice, then spray with satin varnish, or line it with a pretty print paper.

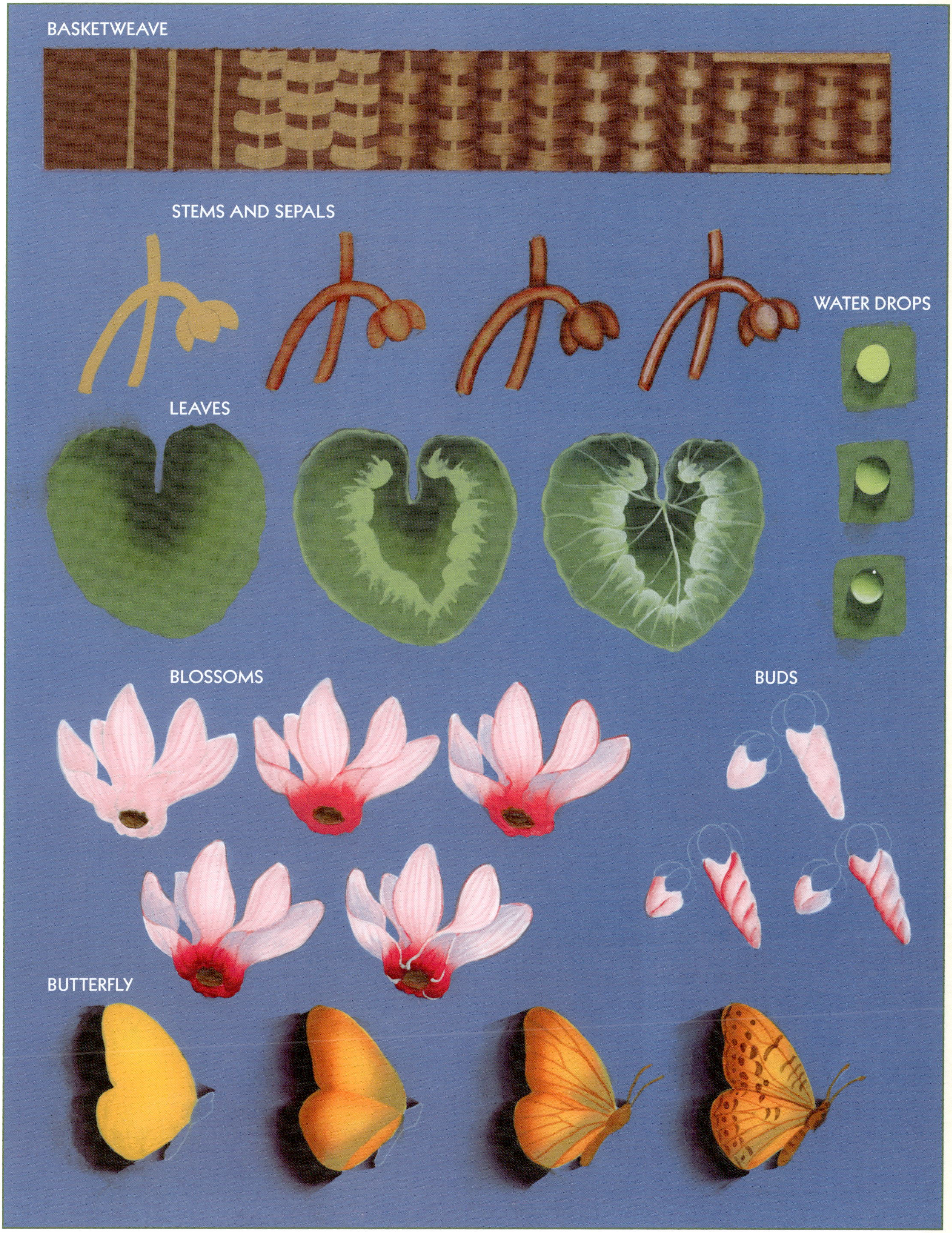
BASKETWEAVE
STEMS AND SEPALS
WATER DROPS
LEAVES
BLOSSOMS
BUDS
BUTTERFLY

Tulip Bucket

Graceful tulips on bent stems adorn this bucket which is perfect as a centerpiece, vase, or for chilling a favorite bottle of wine.

MATERIALS

PALETTE

Delta Ceramcoat Acrylics

- Amethyst
- Antique Gold
- Apple Green
- Bahama Purple
- Black
- Caribbean Blue
- Dark Brown
- Dark Foliage Green
- Heritage Green
- Light Foliage Green
- Light Ivory
- Maroon
- Medium Foliage Green
- Mello Yellow
- Oasis Green
- Old Parchment
- Orange
- Palomino Tan
- Purple
- Tomato Spice
- Yellow

BRUSHES

Loew-Cornell, Inc.

½" and 1½" wash: Series 7550

#4 and #6 shaders: Series 7300

¼", ⅜" and ½" angular shaders: Series 7400

#2 and #4 rounds: Series 7000

#2, #4 and #10 filberts: Series 7500

#0 and #1 liners: Series 7350

SURFACE

French flower bucket, 12" x 7½" (top diameter) x 5" (bottom diameter)

See Resources on page 21

OTHER SUPPLIES

Jo Sonja's Retarder and Antiquing Medium

PATTERN

Refer to pattern on page 20.

PREPARATION

Please read carefully the "General Instructions" in the front of this book before starting this project.

1. Wash with detergent and thoroughly dry the metal container to eliminate any oil or dirt. Brush a coat of *Delta Metal Primer* on the entire outside surface of the container as well as on the inside rim. Let dry.

2. Paint the top rim, as well as the two raised rims close to the top of the container with Bahama Purple. Don't worry if you get some on the main body of the container. It will be covered with other paint. Paint the rim around the bottom of the container with Black.

3. Paint the rest of the outside of the container, except the handles and middle band, with Mello Yellow. Go over the top band with Antique Gold. Paint the band between the two raised rims (see photo) with Black.

4. Shade around the bottom of the container with Antique Gold.

5. Transfer the basic design shapes to the container.

STEMS

1. Basecoat the stems with Oasis Green.

2. Shade the stems on the right side, just below the petals and wherever they come from behind another stem or leaf, with Heritage Green.

3. Deepen the shading with Dark Foliage Green.

4. Highlight with Caribbean Blue.

LEAF

1. Basecoat the top side of the leaf with Oasis Green and the back with Light Foliage Green. Where the leaf grows out of the stem, blend the Light Foliage Green into the stem (see worksheet).

2. Shade the front of the leaf with Heritage Green, down both sides of the center and wherever the back overlaps the front. Shade the front of the leaf on the left side of the stem. Shade the back of the leaf along the folds with Medium Foliage Green.

3. Deepen the shading on the front of the leaf with Dark Foliage Green. Paint very fine lines on the front and back of the leaf with thinned Dark Foliage Green.

4. Highlight between the thin lines on the front of the leaf with Caribbean Blue and on the back with Apple Green.

WATER DROPS

1. Shade around the bottom and partway up the right side of the water drop shapes with Heritage Green, then deepen just under the drop shapes with Dark Foliage Green. Paint the drops with Caribbean Blue.

2. Shade the drops at the top with Heritage Green, and deepen with Dark Foliage Green.

3. Highlight around the bottom with Light Ivory, and add a little highlight dot

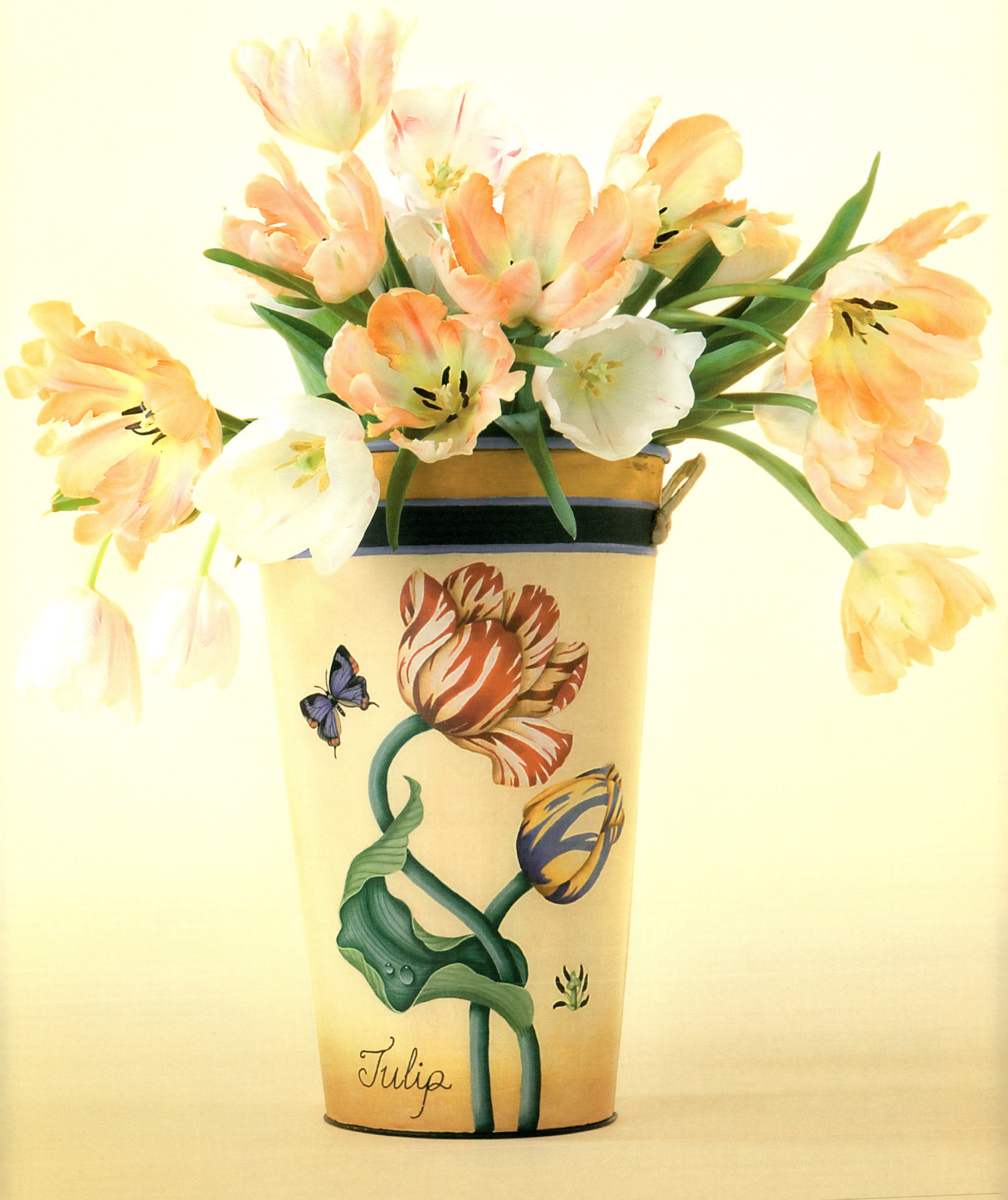
Tulip

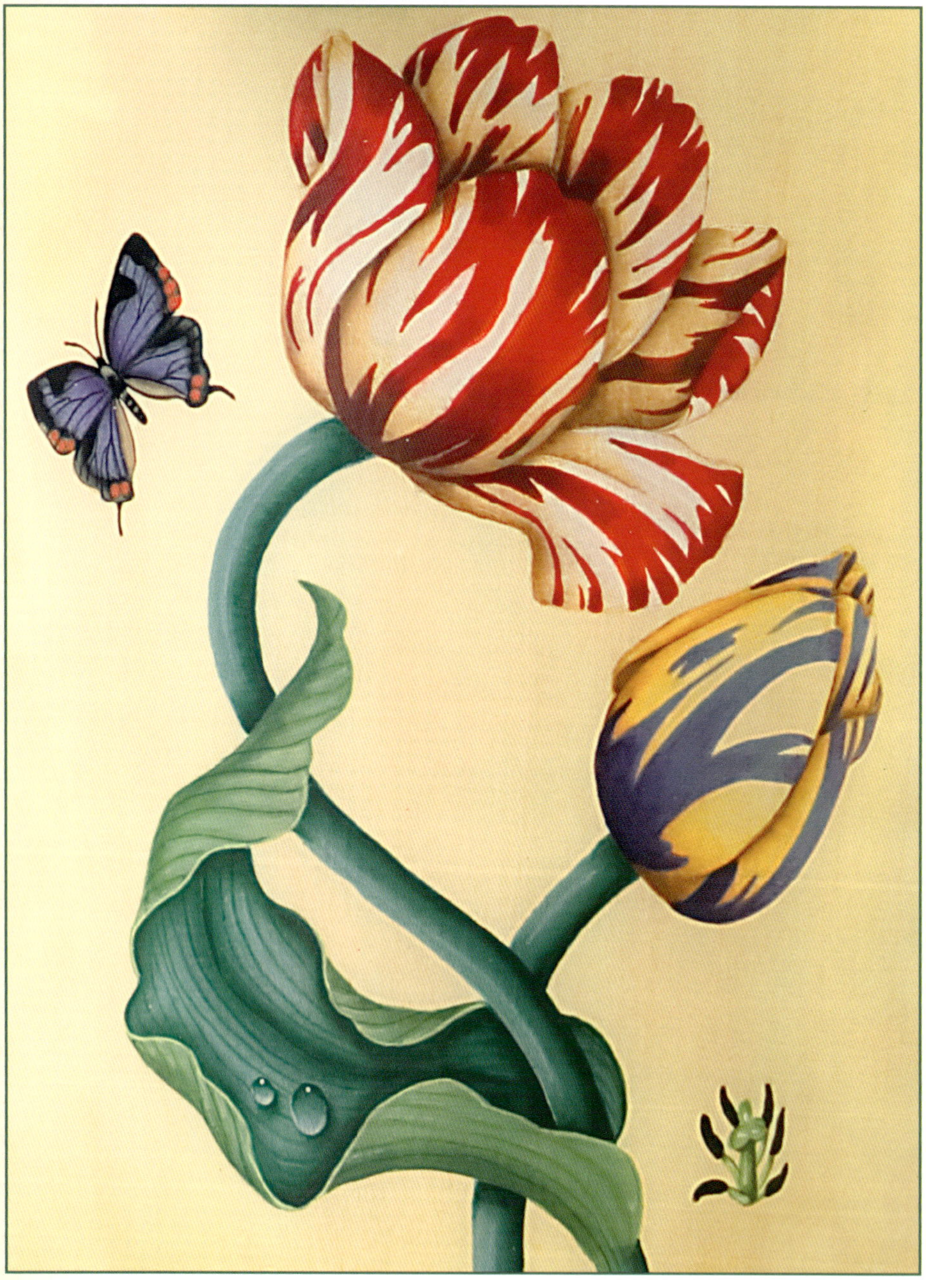

to the darkest area of the top, using the small tip of the stylus and Light Ivory.

RED AND WHITE TULIP

1. Basecoat the entire tulip with Light Ivory, then shade with Old Parchment. Shade around the outside edges of the petals (heavier around the bottom), between the petals and wherever petals overlap.

2. Deepen the shading with Palomino Tan, then a small amount of Dark Brown. The Dark Brown shading should only be around the bottom of the tulip and between the petals and under the overlap, not around the tops of the petals.

3. Paint the stripes with Orange, then shade with Tomato Spice. The shading on the stripes should be in the same areas as the shading on the white areas of the tulip.

4. Deepen the shading on the stripes with Maroon, then highlight the white areas with Light Ivory (see worksheet).

PURPLE AND YELLOW TULIP

1. Shade the tulip with Yellow in the same manner as the red and white tulip, and deepen with Antique Gold.

2. Further deepen the shading with a small amount of Dark Brown.

3. Paint the stripes with Bahama Purple and shade with Amethyst.

4. Deepen the shading with Purple.

STAMENS AND ANTHERS

1. Basecoat with Apple Green.

2. Shade with Light Foliage Green and deepen the stamen just below the tri-section top with Medium Foliage Green (see worksheet).

3. Highlight with Light Ivory.

4. Paint the six side anthers with Black.

BUTTERFLY

1. Basecoat the wings with Bahama Purple, then glaze with Amethyst.

2. Shade close to the body with Purple, then paint the section on the lower wings closest to the body with Palomino Tan.

3. Paint the body, antennae, and dark areas on the wings with Black. Soften by shading around the edges where the Black meets the Bahama Purple and Palomino Tan.

4. Highlight the Black on the body and wings with Palomino Tan, then add the Black veins. Add Orange spots where indicated.

FINISHING

1. With the black permanent ink fine-line pen, trace over the word "Tulip."

2. Erase any remaining transfer lines.

3. Antique the container by brushing on a coat of *Jo Sonja's Retarder and Antiquing Medium* and then immediately brush on a coat of Dark Brown. Wipe off with a soft cloth.

4. Let dry thoroughly, and spray with satin varnish.

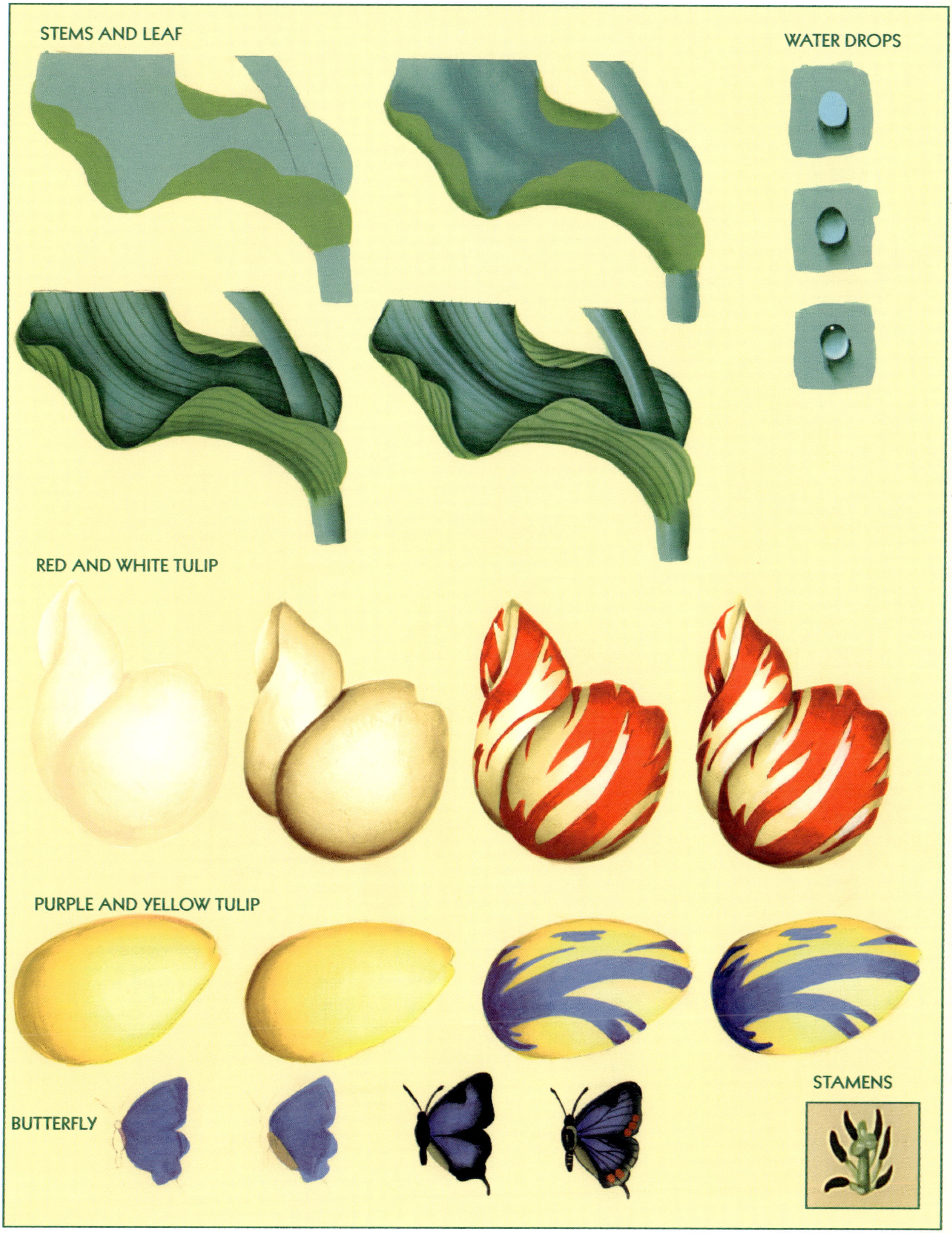
STEMS AND LEAF
WATER DROPS
RED AND WHITE TULIP
PURPLE AND YELLOW TULIP
BUTTERFLY
STAMENS

Fruit Ovals

MATERIALS

PALETTE

Delta Ceramcoat Acrylics

Amethyst
Antique White
Apple Green
Autumn Brown
Avocado
Black
Black Cherry
Blue Heaven
Blue Jay
Bright Red
Brown Velvet
Burnt Umber
Caribbean Blue
Copen Blue
Dark Foliage Green
Deep Lilac
Egg Plant
Lemon Grass
Light Foliage Green
Light Timberline Green
Lilac Dusk
Maple Sugar Tan
Maroon
Medium Foliage Green
Moroccan Red
Ocean Reef Blue
Old Parchment
Orange
Spice Tan
Terra Cotta
Timberline Green
Toffee Brown
Vintage Wine
White

BRUSHES

Loew-Cornell, Inc.

1" and 1½" wash: Series 7550
#0 and #1 liners: Series 7350
#4 and #8 shaders: Series 7300
¼", ⅜" and ½" angular shaders: Series 7400
#2, #4, #6 and #8 filberts: Series 7500

SURFACE

Basswood oval, 9" x 12" (item #1839, *Walnut Hollow)*
See Resources on page 21

OTHER SUPPLIES

Delta Fine Crackle Finish, Steps 1 and 2
Delta Gel Stain Medium
Decorative hangers

Hang these luscious red currants and juicy purple plums in your home to celebrate the fruits of summer.

PLUMS OVAL

PATTERN

Refer to center insert.

PREPARATION

Please read carefully the "General Instructions" in the front of the book before starting this project.

1. Basecoat the top of the plaque with Antique White. Transfer the oval shape to the top and shade just inside this with Old Parchment, then deepen with Maple Sugar Tan.

2. Basecoat the rim around the oval with Maple Sugar Tan. Paint the sides and back of the plaque with Terra Cotta.

3. Transfer the basic design outlines.

BRANCH

1. Basecoat the branch with Toffee Brown. With Autumn Brown, shade the left side of the branch, around the cut edge and around and on the left or lower side of the nodules. Add an Autumn Brown center to the empty nodule on the right side of the branch.

2. Deepen the shading with Brown Velvet.

3. Highlight a little to the right of center with Spice Tan. Paint the cut edge with Light Timberline Green, and add a tiny Timberline Green accent in the center.

LEAVES AND STEMS

Fronts

1. Paint the stems (except the stems to top two leaves) and the front of the leaves with Light Foliage Green. With Medium Foliage Green, shade around the leaf edges, down both sides of the center vein, and below the side veins. On the lower three small leaves, shade wherever they overlap. Shade the stems where they come out of the branch.

2. Deepen the shading on the left side of the center vein and below the side veins with Dark Foliage Green; deepen the shading on the overlapped areas of the lower leaves.

3. Paint the veins with Apple Green. At the same time, paint a fine Apple Green line around the overlapping leaf edges and around the edge of the leaf which overlaps the branch.

4. Highlight between the veins with Caribbean Blue.

LEAF BACKS AND STEMS

1. Basecoat the leaf backs and the stems on the top two leaves with Light Timberline Green.

2. Shade above the vein lines and on both sides of the center vein with Timberline Green.

3. Paint the vein lines with Avocado.

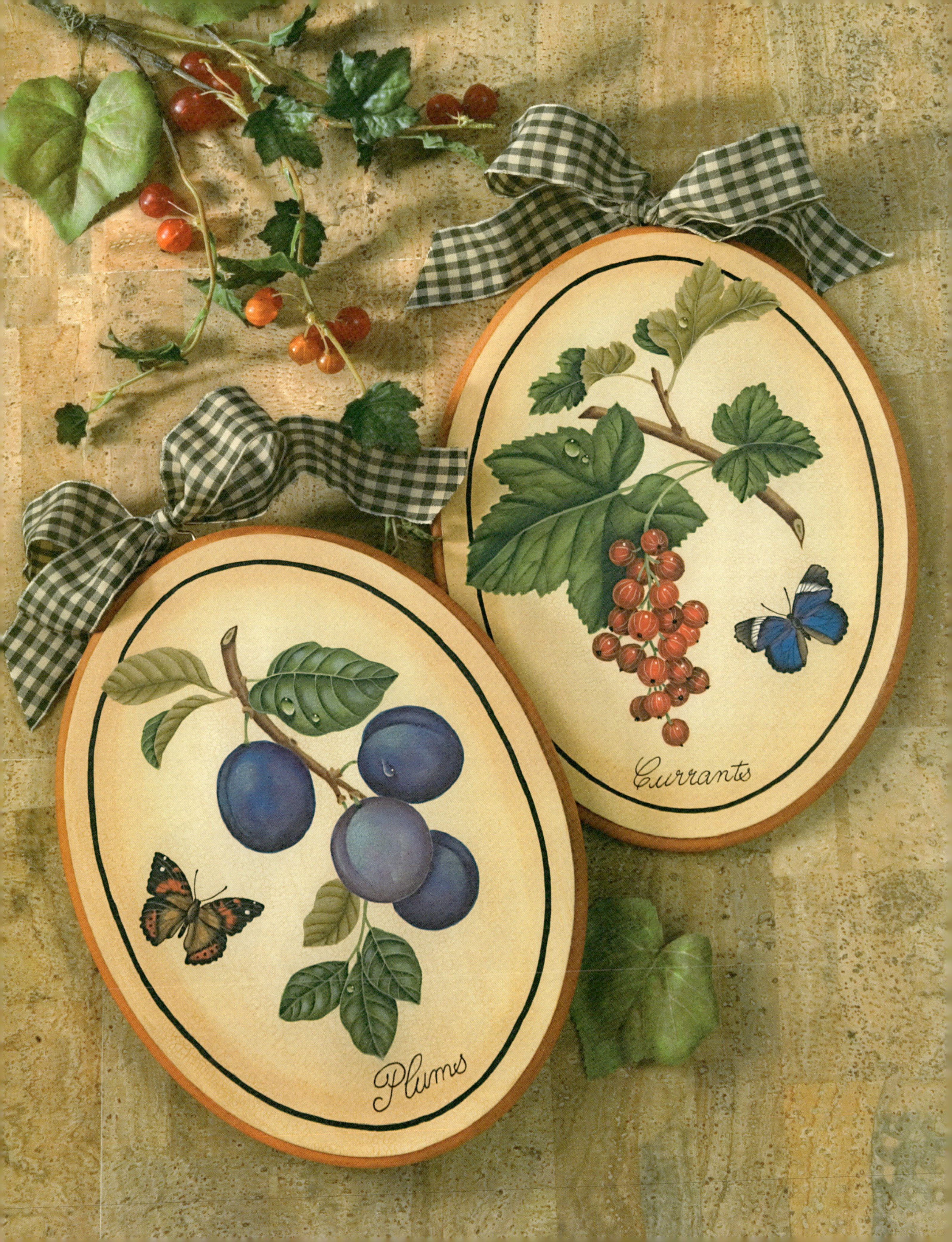
Currants
Plums

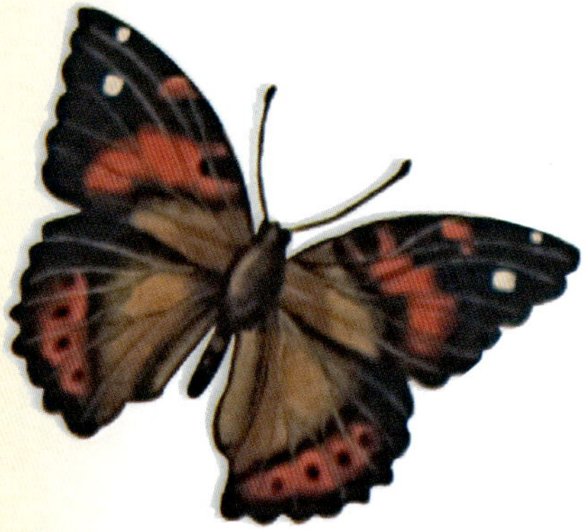

WATER DROPS ON LEAVES

1. Shade around the bottom and partway up the left side of the drop shapes with Dark Foliage Green. Paint the drops with Apple Green.
2. Shade the drops on the top right with Medium Foliage Green, then deepen at the top with Dark Foliage Green.
3. Highlight around the bottom and left side with White. Add a small White highlight to the top with the small stylus tip.

DARK PLUMS

1. Basecoat the three dark plums with Ocean Reef Blue, then glaze with a mix of Gel Stain Medium + Egg Plant (2:1), keeping it heavier around the edges and the small side of the indentation. While wet, pat with a soft cloth or paper towel on the fat side of the indentation to remove a little of the glaze.
2. Shade around the edges of the plums and in the indentations with Vintage Wine.
3. With the #8 filbert, add accents by patting on some Deep Lilac.
4. Highlight with Blue Jay (see worksheet).

WATER DROP ON PLUM

1. Shade around the bottom and left side of the drop shape with Vintage Wine. Paint the drop with Ocean Reef Blue, blending the top of the drop into the plum.
2. Shade on the right side with Egg Plant, then deepen the shading with Vintage Wine.
3. Highlight down the left side and around the bottom with White, then add a tiny dot of White to the lower right side.

LIGHT PLUM

1. Basecoat with Blue Jay. Glaze with a mix of Gel Stain Medium + Deep Lilac (2:1) and pat, the same as with the dark plums.
2. Shade with a mix of Amethyst + Lilac Dusk (2:1), then pat on some Lilac Dusk accents.
3. Highlight with Blue Heaven. Paint a fine line where the light plum and the dark plum overlap with Blue Heaven.

BUTTERFLY

1. Basecoat the butterfly wings with Spice Tan, Orange, and Black, in the spaces indicated on the worksheet. Paint the body and antennae Black.
2. With Autumn Brown, shade close to the body on the upper wings and alongside the segment closest to the body on the lower wings. Shade the orange section, next to the Black, with Bright Red.
3. Shade under the upper wings and down the light segment of the lower wings with Black. Also with Black, shade around the red and tan areas to soften.
4. Paint the veins through light areas of the wings with Black, then alongside these lines and through the Black areas with Toffee Brown. Paint a fine line all around the outside of the wings with Black.
5. Highlight the body with Autumn

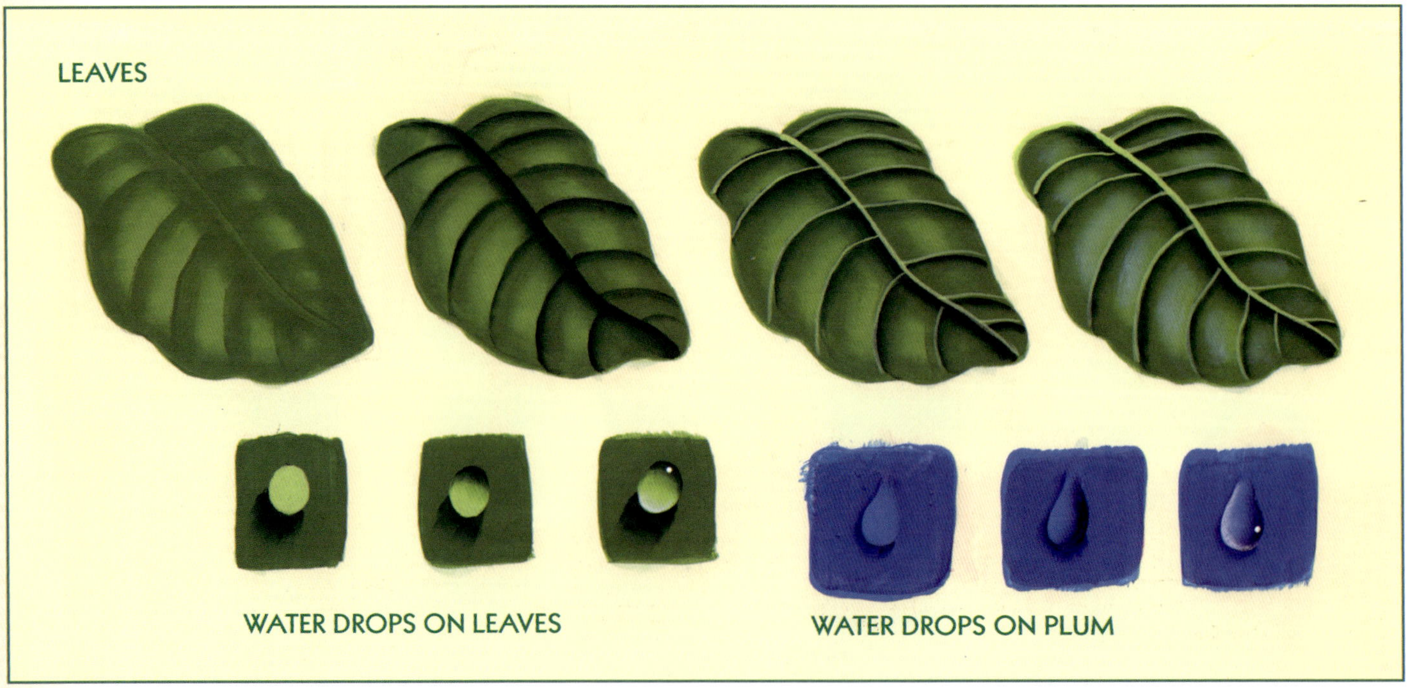

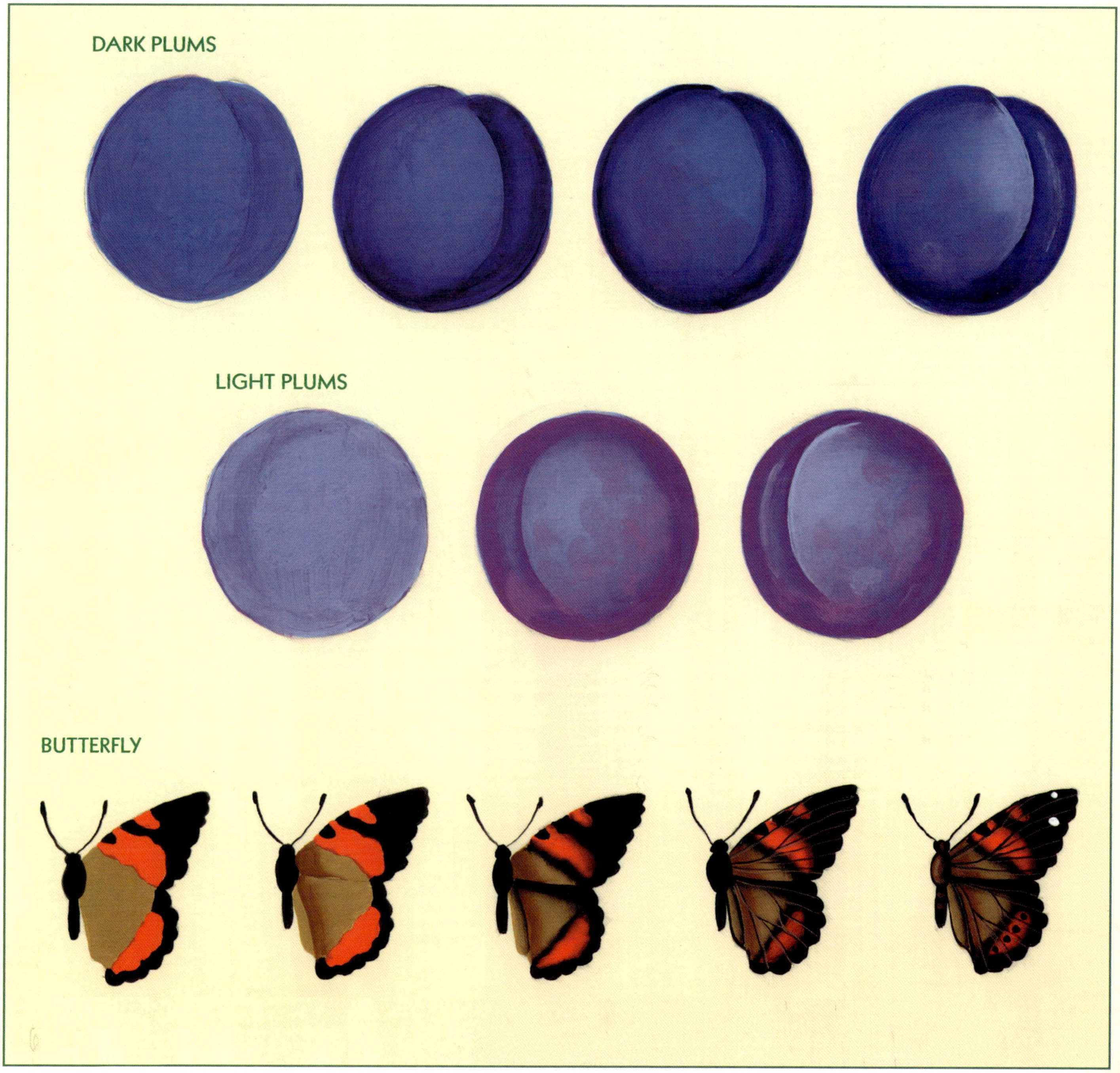

Brown, and add a small highlight on top of this with Toffee Brown. Add the White accents to the upper wings and the Black accents to the lower wings.

FINISHING

1. Paint the line around the inside oval with Black, and trace the word "Plums" with the black permanent ink fine-line pen.

2. Erase any remaining transfer lines.

3. Following the directions on the bottles carefully, brush on Step 1 of the *Delta Fine Crackle Finish* (keeping in mind that the thicker Step 1 is brushed on, the larger the cracks. Varying the thickness of Step 1 gives a more realistic and interesting look). When dry, brush on Step 2. Dry overnight.

4. Brush a mix of Gel Stain Medium + Burnt Umber (2:1) over the top of the plaque, then immediately wipe off with a soft cloth.

5. When thoroughly dry, spray with a couple of coats of satin varnish.

6. Add a decorative hanger to the top of the plaque, hang, and enjoy.

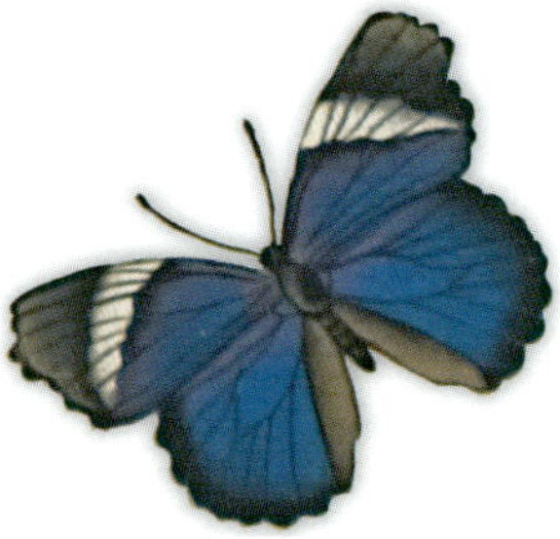

CURRANTS OVAL

MATERIALS

PALETTE

Delta Ceramcoat Acrylics

Antique White
Apple Green
Autumn Brown
Avocado
Black
Black Cherry
Bright Red
Brown Velvet
Burnt Umber
Copen Blue
Dark Foliage Green
Deep Lilac
Lemon Grass
Light Foliage Green
Light Timberline Green
Maple Sugar Tan
Maroon
Medium Foliage Green
Moroccan Red
Orange
Spice Tan
Terra Cotta
Timberline Green
Toffee Brown
White

BRUSHES

Loew-Cornell, Inc.

1" and 1½" wash: Series 7550
#0 and #1 liners: Series 7350
#4 and #8 shaders: Series 7300
¼", ⅜" and ½" angular shaders: Series 7400
#2, #4, #6 and #8 filberts: Series 7500

SURFACE

Basswood oval, 9" x 12" (item #1839, *Walnut Hollow)*

See Resources on page 21

OTHER SUPPLIES

Delta Fine Crackle Finish, Steps 1 and 2
Delta Gel Stain Medium
Decorative Hangers

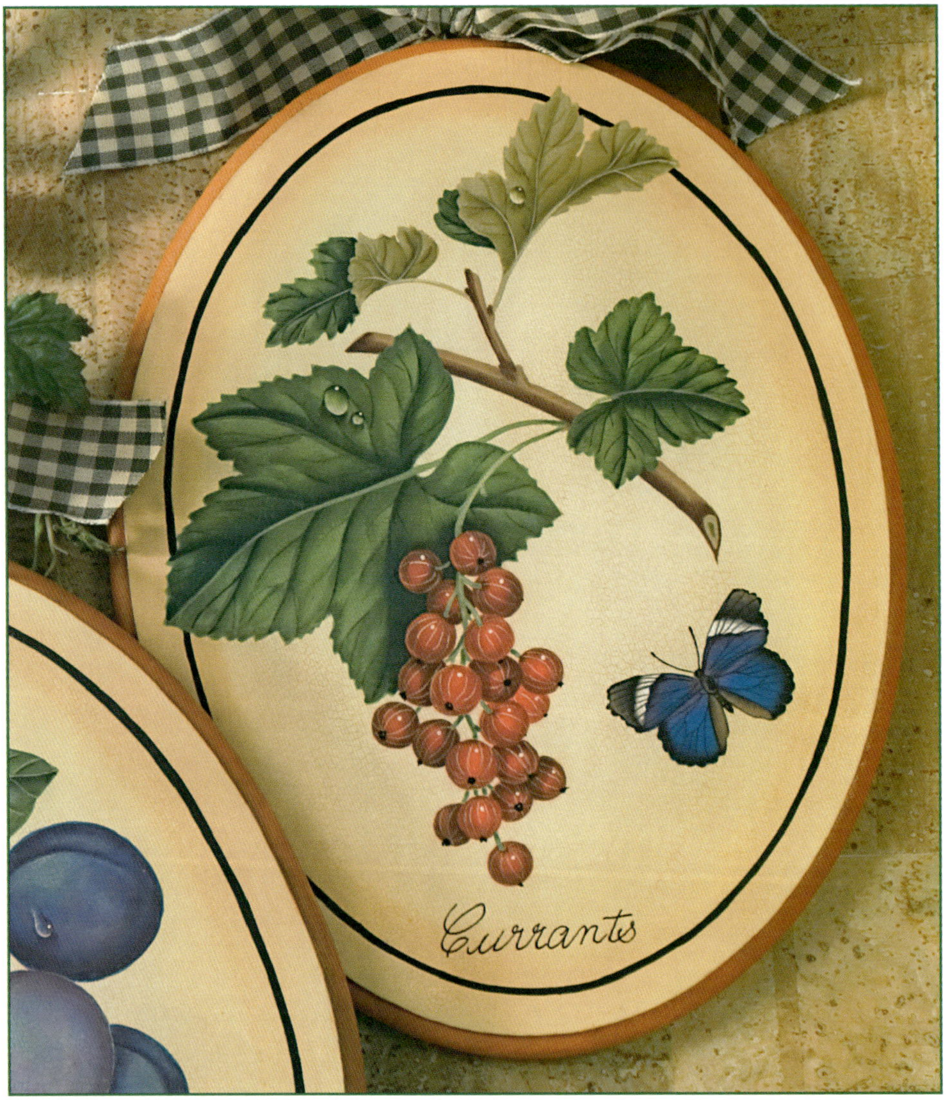

PATTERN

Refer to center insert.

PREPARATION

Please read carefully the "General Instructions" in the front of the book before starting this project.

1. Basecoat the top of the plaque with Antique White. Transfer the oval shape to the top and shade just inside this with Old Parchment, then deepen with Maple Sugar Tan.

2. Basecoat the rim around the oval with Maple Sugar Tan. Paint the side and back of the plaque with Terra Cotta.

3. Transfer the basic design outlines to the plaque.

BRANCHES

1. Basecoat the branches with Toffee Brown. Shade the lower side of the branches, around the cut edge, and where the small branch grows out of the main branch, with Autumn Brown.

2. Deepen the shading with Brown Velvet.

3. Highlight a little to the right of center with Spice Tan. Paint the cut edge with Light Timberline Green with a tiny Timberline Green accent in the center.

LEAVES

Front

1. Basecoat the stems and the front of the leaves with Light Foliage Green.

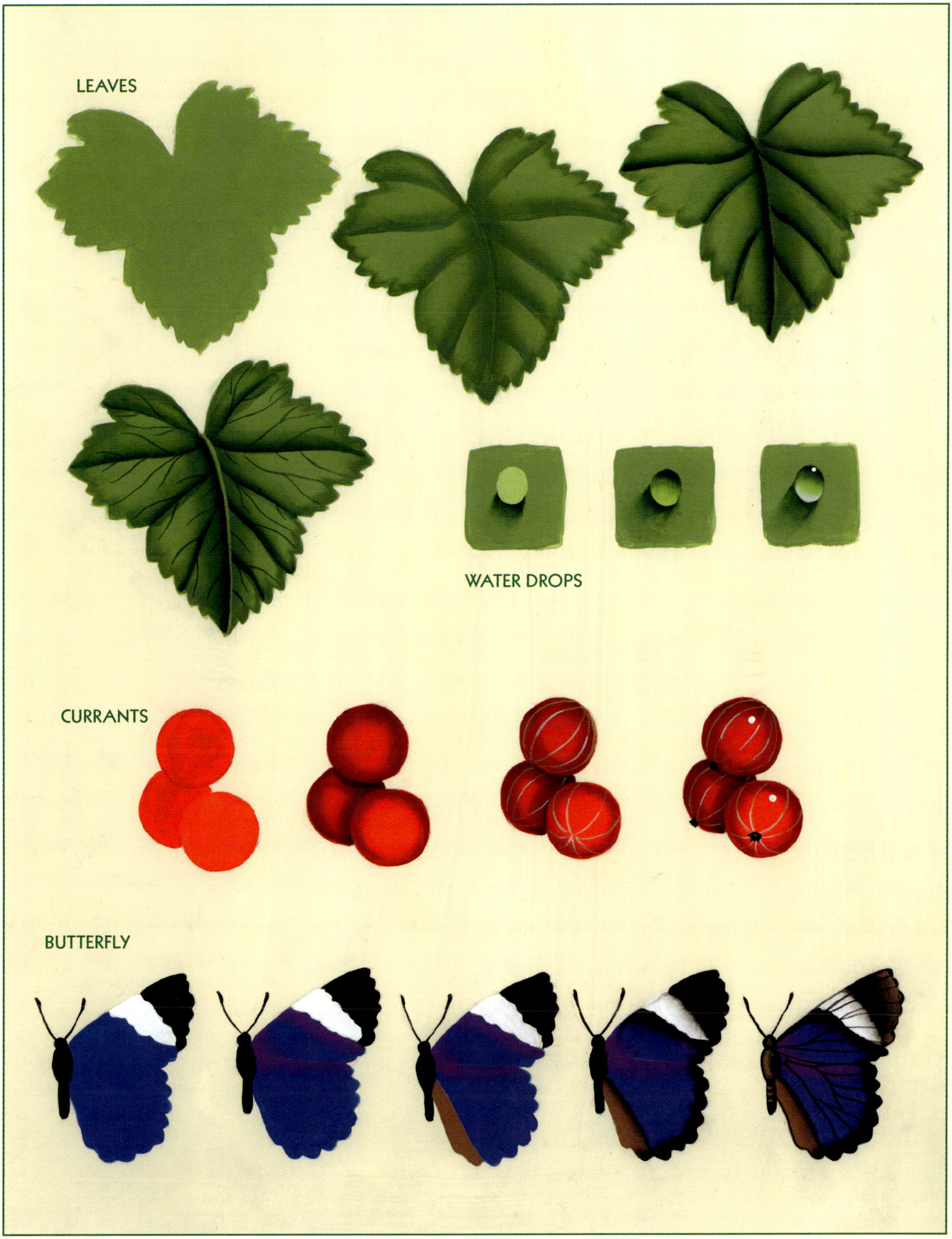
LEAVES
WATER DROPS
CURRANTS
BUTTERFLY

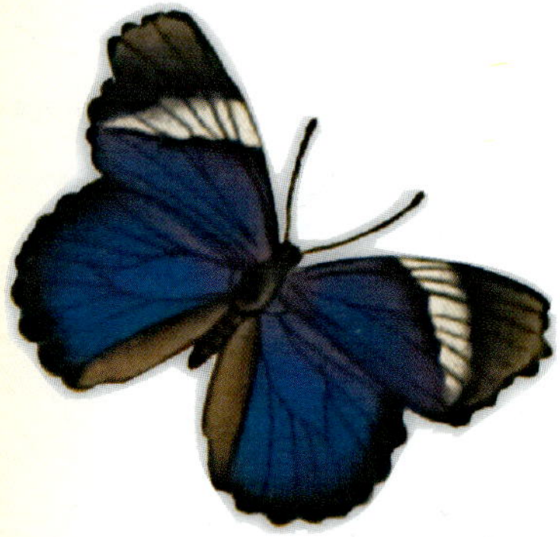

2. With Medium Foliage Green, shade around the outside of the leaves, on both sides of the center vein, above the main side vein lines, and around the edge of the currants on the large leaf. On the large leaf only, shade above the small vein lines.
3. With Dark Foliage Green, deepen the shading on the left side of the center vein and above the large side veins, around the currants on the large leaf, and under the overlap on the two top leaves.
4. With Dark Foliage Green, paint the small veins coming off the large side veins, then paint the center vein with Light Foliage Green.

Back

1. Basecoat the leaf backs with Light Timberline Green. Shade on both sides of the center vein and above the side veins with Timberline Green.
2. With Avocado, deepen the shading below the center vein line and above the main side veins. Paint the small side veins also with Avocado.
3. With Lemon Grass, paint the center vein and main side veins.

WATER DROPS

On Front of Leaf

1. Shade around the bottom and partway up the left side of the drop shape with Dark Foliage Green. Paint the drops with Apple Green.
2. Shade the drop shape on the top right with Medium Foliage Green, followed by Dark Foliage Green at the top.
3. Highlight around the bottom and left side with White. Make a tiny White highlight dot in the darkest area of the top with the small stylus tip.

WATER DROP

On Back of Leaf

1. Paint according to the directions for the water dross on the front of the leaves, shading under the drop shape with Avocado.
2. Paint the drop with Lemon Grass, shade with Timberline Green and Avocado, and highlight with White.

CURRANTS

1. There are darker currants and lighter currants. Basecoat the darker currants with Bright Red and the lighter currants with Orange.
Note: Basecoat the currants over the large leaf with White first; when dry, basecoat with Bright Red. The bunch of currants is easier to paint if you paint the dark currants first, through Step 2, before starting the lighter currants. At this point, you probably will have gotten paint on the light currants, and if this is the case you will need to basecoat them with White before painting with Orange.
2. Shade the darker currants all around the edges with Maroon, followed by Black Cherry where they are behind other currants. Shade the lighter currants with Moroccan Red.
3. Paint the thin lines through the currants with Spice Tan, then highlight the lines in the center of the currants with White.
4. Paint the little ends of the currants with Black. Highlight the currants with a dot of White.

BUTTERFLY

1. Basecoat the blue area of the wings with Copen Blue and the white area with White. Paint the top wing tips, the body, and the antennae with Black.
2. Shade the upper wings close to the body and next to the White area with Deep Lilac. On the lower wings, shade the area below the upper wings with Deep Lilac.
3. Paint the section on the lower wings closest to the body with Toffee Brown.
4. On the upper wings, soften the edge between the White and Black with a thin shading of Black. Add a thin Black shading between the White and Deep Lilac area, heavier toward the top of the wings. On the lower wings, soften the line between the Toffee Brown and Copen Blue in the same way. Add a shading of Black around the outside edges of the lower wings and the lower edge of the upper wings.
5. Highlight the body and the Black tips on the upper wings with Toffee Brown, then paint the vein lines with Black. Paint a very thin line around the upper and lower wings with Black.

FINISHING

1. Paint the line around the inside oval with Black, and trace the word "Currants" with the black permanent ink fine-line pen.
2. Following the directions on the bottles carefully, brush on Step 1 of the *Delta Fine Crackle Finish* (keeping in mind that the thicker Step 1 is brushed on, the larger the cracks. Varying the thickness of Step 1 gives a more realistic and interesting look). When dry, brush on Step 2. Dry overnight.
3. Brush a mix of Gel Stain Medium + Burnt Umber (2:1) over the top of the plaque, then immediately wipe off with a soft cloth.
4. When thoroughly dry, spray with a couple of coats of satin varnish.
5. Add a decorative hanger to the top of the plaque, hang, and enjoy.

project on page 4

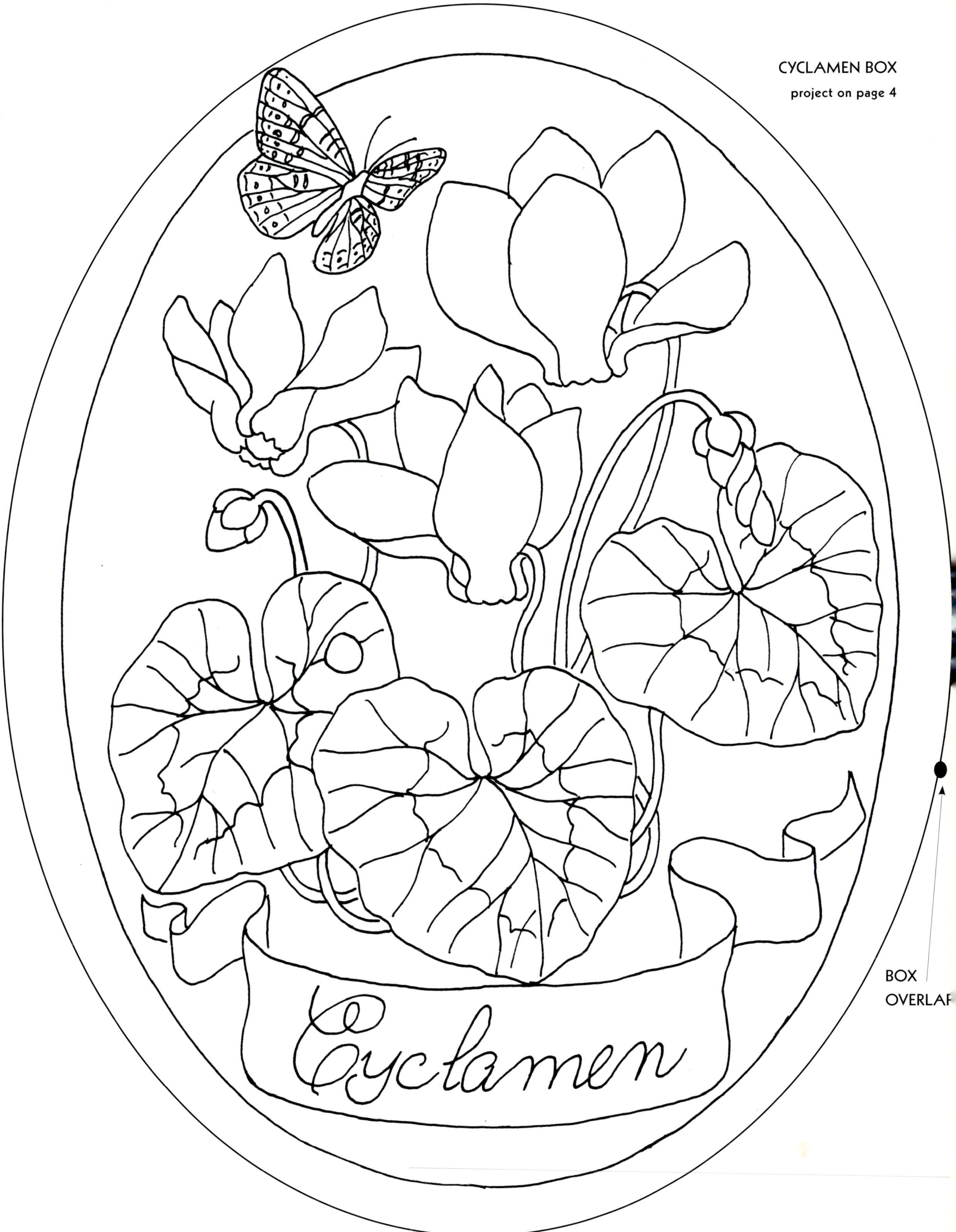

TULIP BUCKET

project on page 8

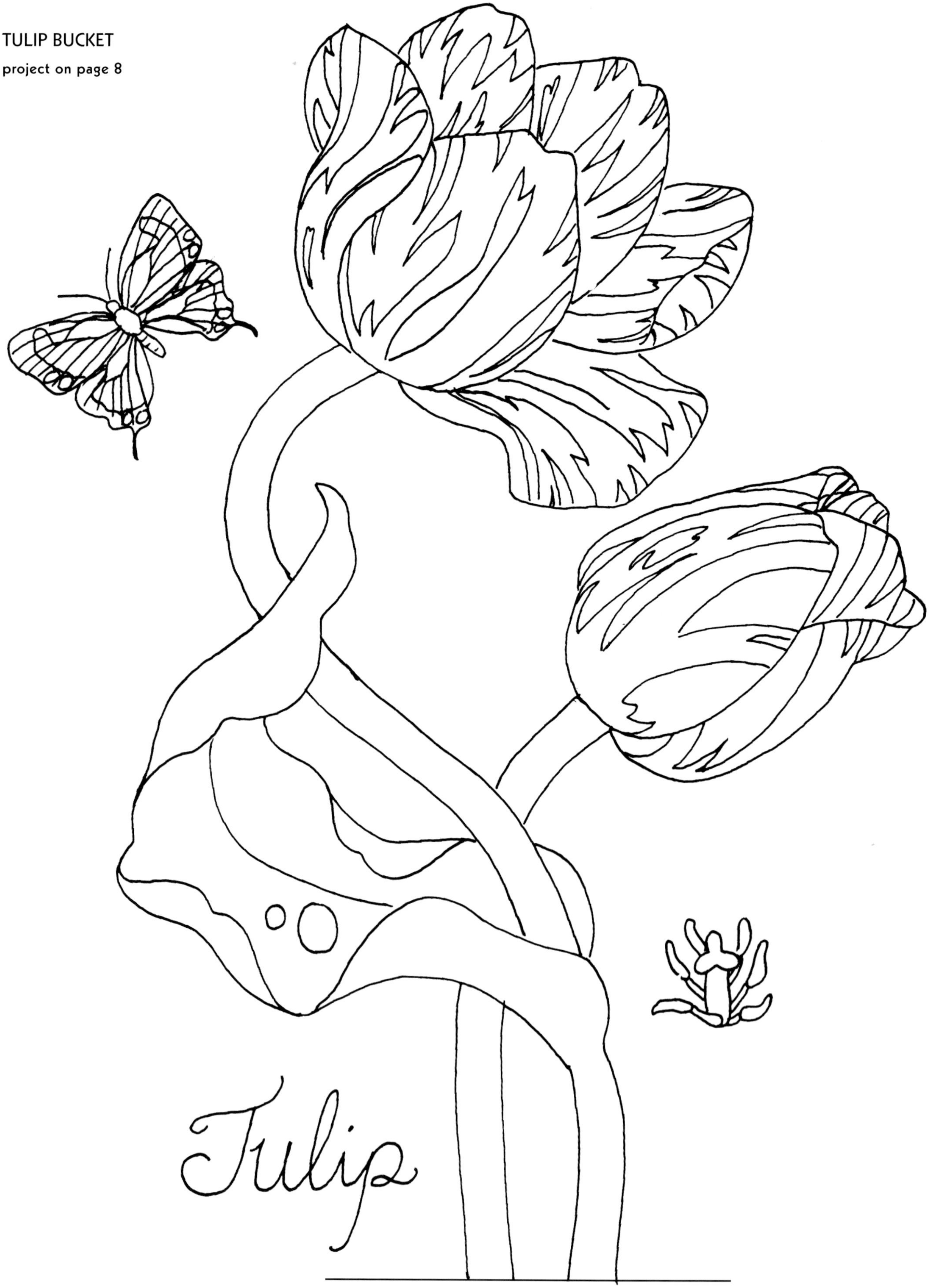

Resources

Most products used to create the designs in the book are available at your local craft retailer. For specialty surfaces/supplies or assistance in locating a retailer, consult the companies below.

3M CO.
Superfine Sanding Sponge
3M Center Building 223-3NE-07
St. Paul, MN 55144-1001
651-736-2371
www.3m.com

DELTA TECHNICAL COATINGS
Delta Ceramcoat
2550 Pellissier Pl.
Whittier, CA 90601
800-423-4135
www.deltacrafts.com

CHROMA INC.
Jo Sonja Products
205 Bucky Dr.
Lititz, PA 17543-7600
717-626-8866
www.ChromaOnline.com

HOFCRAFT
P.O. Box 72
Grand Haven, MI 49417
800-828-0359
www.hofcraft.com

LOEW-CORNELL, INC
563 Chestnut Ave.
Teaneck, NJ 07666
201-836-7070
loew-cornell@lowe-cornell.com
www.loew-cornell.com

MASTERSON ART PRODUCTS, INC.
Masterson's Sta-Wet Palette
P.O. Box 10775
Glendale, AZ 85318
602-263-6017
www.mastersonart.com

ROYAL & LANGNICKEL
BRUSH MANUFACTURING, INC.
6707 Broadway
Merrillville, IN 46410
800-247-2211
www.royalbrush.com

WALNUT HOLLOW
1409 State Road 23
Dodgeville, WI 53533
800-950-5101
www.walnuthollow.com

FIG BASKET

project on page 28

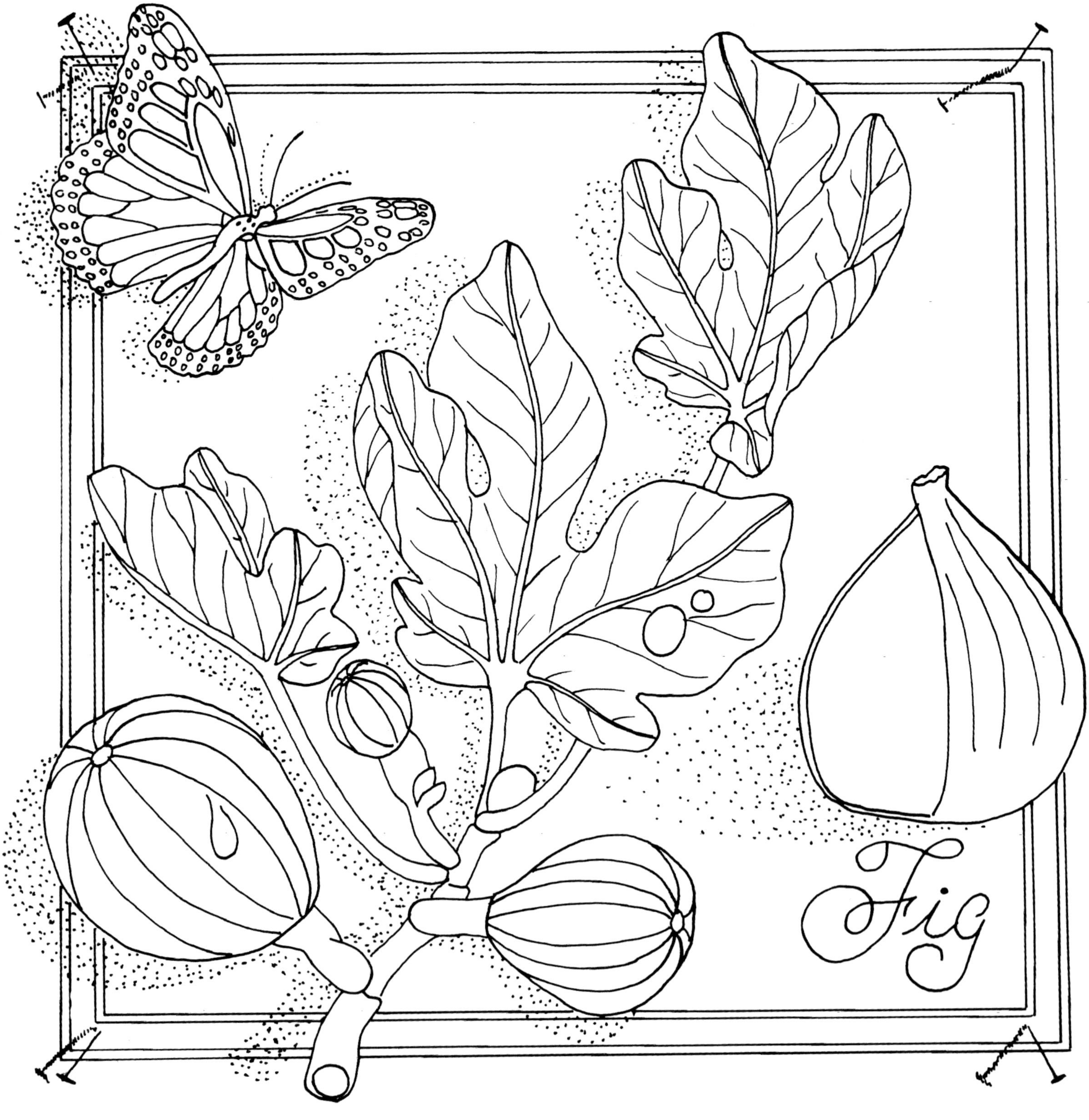

project on page 24

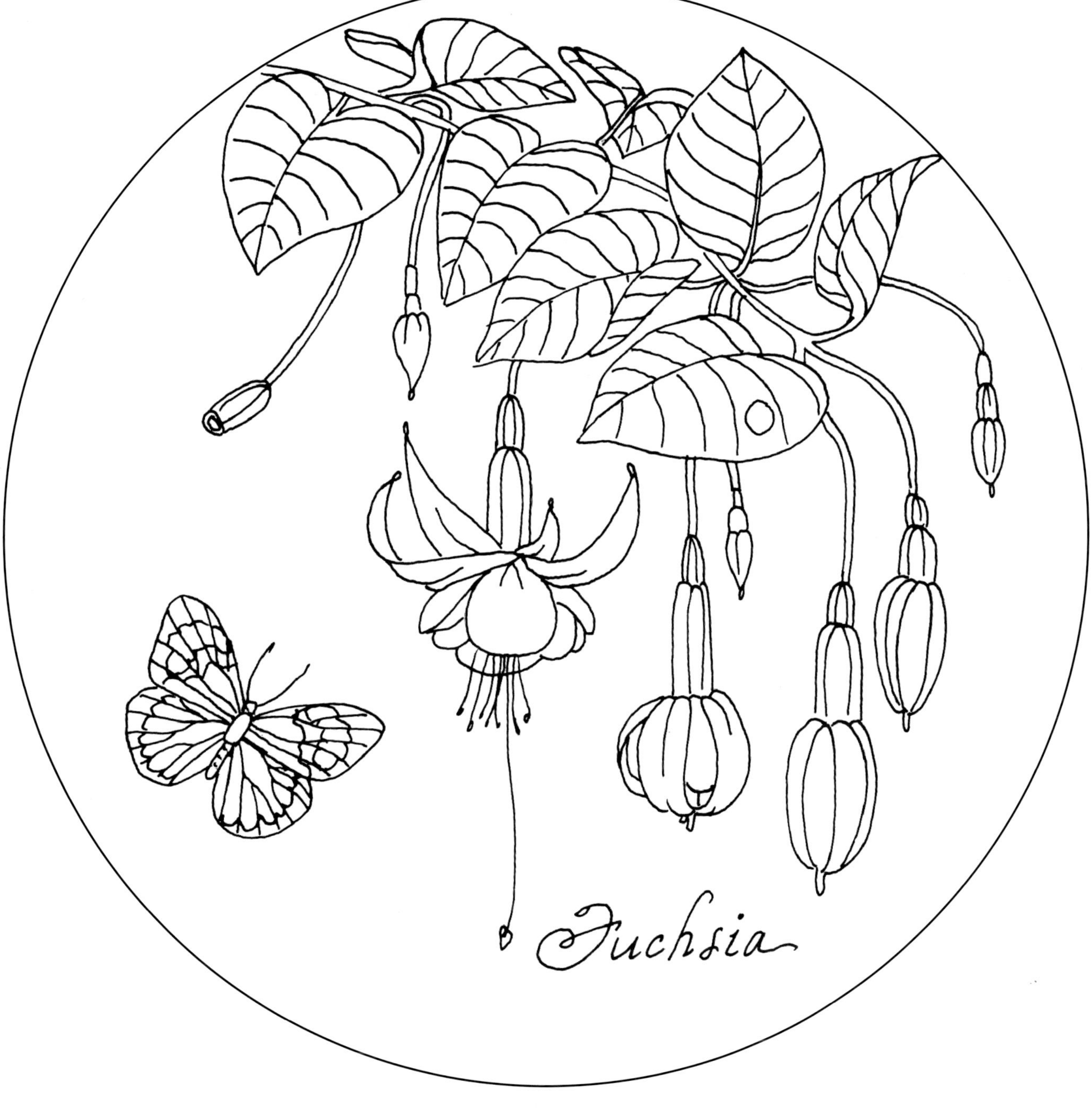

Fuchsia Box

Reminiscent of elegant dancing garden ballerinas, you can enjoy the delicate beauty of these brightly colored flowers all year long on this graceful scalloped-edged box.

MATERIALS

PALETTE

Delta Ceramcoat Acrylics

Apple Green	Moroccan Red
Black	Napthol Crimson
Black Cherry	Oasis Green
Chambray Blue	Peony
Dark Foliage Green	Pink Quartz
Fuchsia	Pumpkin
Heritage Green	Raw Sienna
Light Foliage Green	Tangerine
Light Ivory	Tidepool Blue
Maple Sugar Tan	
Medium Foliage Green	

BRUSHES

Loew-Cornell, Inc.

½" and 1" wash: Series 7550

¼", ½" and ¾" angular shaders: Series 7400

#2, #6 and #8 filberts: Series 7500

#10/0 and #2 liners: Series 7350

SURFACE

Large circle box, 7¼" x 2¼" x 7¼" (item #24062, *Walnut Hollow*)

See Resources on page 21

PATTERN

Refer to the pattern on page 23.

PREPARATION

Please read carefully the "General Instructions" in the front of the book before starting this project.

1. Stain the entire box with a very thin coat of Heritage Green, allowing the wood grain to show through.

2. Over this, add a thin glaze of Light Ivory. Allow to dry, then spatter with Black, using an old toothbrush.

3. When the box is thoroughly dry, sand with a plain paper bag to smooth the grain, then spray with matte varnish.

4. Transfer the basic design shapes to the top.

MAIN STEM

1. Paint the main large stem with Medium Foliage Green.

2. Shade on the lower side and wherever it appears from behind a leaf with some thinned Black Cherry (see worksheet on page 27).

LEAVES, FLOWER STEMS, AND TOPS OF FUCHSIAS

1. Basecoat the front of the leaves, the stems, and the green tops of the fuchsias with Light Foliage Green. Basecoat the backs of the leaves with Oasis Green. Shade the front of the leaves, the stems, and the green tops of the fuchsias with Medium Foliage Green (see photo and worksheet for placement). Shade the back of the leaves with Heritage Green.

2. Deepen the shading on the front and back of the leaves, as well as the stems and the green tops of the fuchsias, with Dark Foliage Green.

3. Highlight the front of the leaves with Oasis Green and the stems and tops of the fuchsias with Apple Green.

4. Add vein lines to the front of the leaves with Apple Green. Add little spiky edges to the front of the leaves with Apple Green. Paint the vein lines and spiky edges on the back of the leaves with Dark Foliage Green, except on the leaves where the back is turned over the front. Paint these spiky edges with Oasis Green.

WATER DROP

1. Shade around the bottom and partway up the left side of the drop shape with Medium Foliage Green, then add a deeper shading of Dark Foliage Green. Paint the drop with Apple Green.

2. Shade the drop on the top and a bit to the right with Medium Foliage Green, deepened at the top with Dark Foliage Green.

3. Highlight around the bottom with Light Ivory, and add a tiny highlight dot to the darkest area of the top with Light Ivory, using the smallest tip of the stylus.

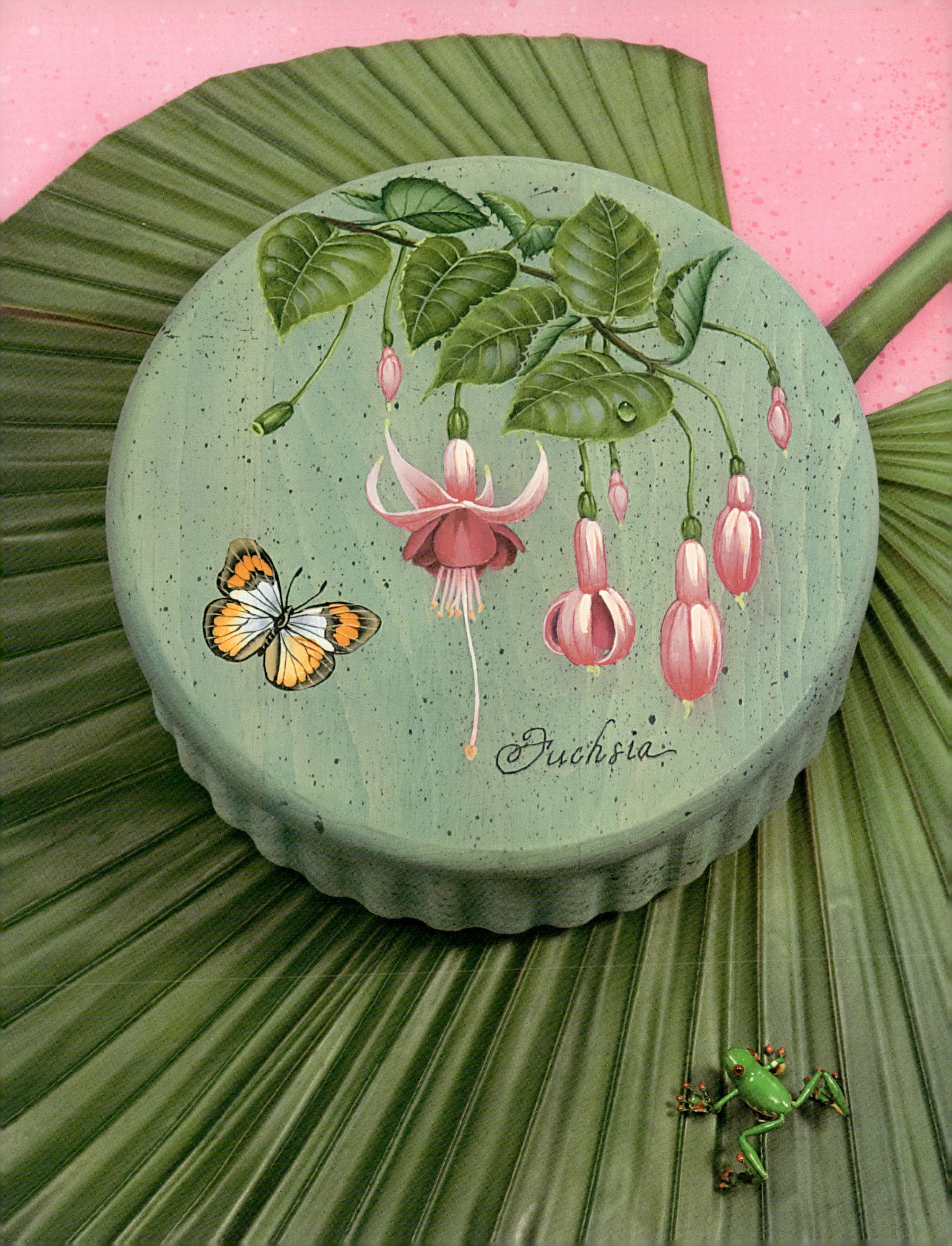
Fuchsia

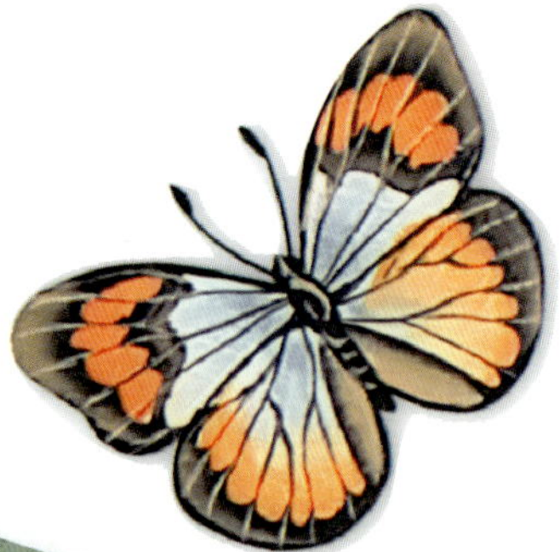

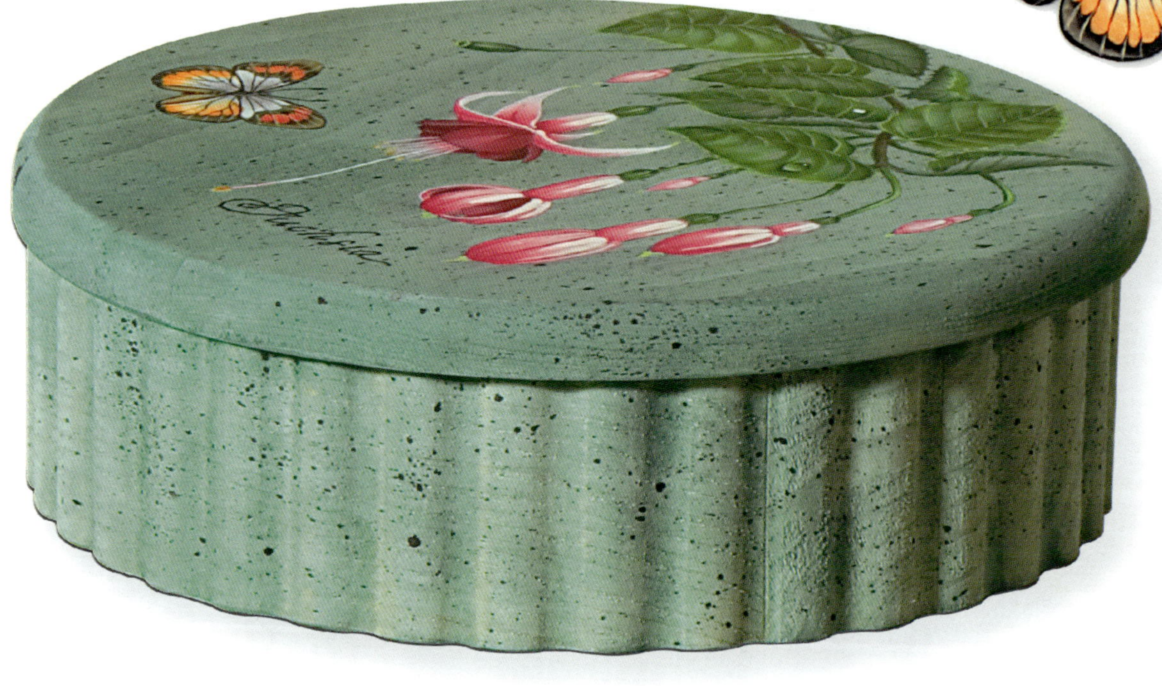

FUCHSIA BLOSSOMS

Lower Petals

1. Basecoat the lower petals with Fuchsia; shade with Napthol Crimson (see worksheet).

2. Deepen the shading with Moroccan Red.

3. Add details with Black Cherry.

Upper Petals

1. Basecoat the upper petals with Peony, shaded with Pink Quartz (see worksheet.)

2. Deepen the shading with Fuchsia, and add details with Napthol Crimson.

3. Highlight with Peony.

4. Further highlight with Light Ivory in a few places (see photo), then add little Apple Green tips.

Stamens

1. Paint the short stamens with a mix of Peony + Pink Quartz (1:1). Paint the long center stamen with Peony (see photo).

2. Shade the stamens, where they come out of the petals, with Fuchsia; shade the lower end of the long center stamen with Fuchsia.

3. Paint the anthers (tips) with Maple Sugar Tan. Add a tiny bit of shading on the left with Raw Sienna.

BUTTERFLY

1. Basecoat the wings with Light Ivory. Shade the wings close to the body with Chambray Blue, deepened with a small amount of Tidepool Blue.

2. Paint the orange area on the top wing with Pumpkin; shade around the outside edge with Tangerine. On the lower wings, shade around the outside edge of the Light Ivory with Pumpkin.

3. Paint the section closest to the body on the lower wing with Maple Sugar Tan, then shade along the vein line with a small amount of Black to soften.

4. Paint the body and the dark parts of the wings with Black. Also with Black, paint the antennae, the veins going through the light areas of the wings, and a fine line around the outside of the Maple Sugar Tan section.

5. Highlight the body with Maple Sugar Tan. Highlight the edges of the Black areas on the wings (see worksheet) and paint the vein lines through the dark areas of the wings with Maple Sugar Tan.

FINISHING

1. With the black permanent ink fine-line pen, trace over the "Fuchsia" lettering.

2. Erase any remaining transfer lines, and spray with satin varnish.

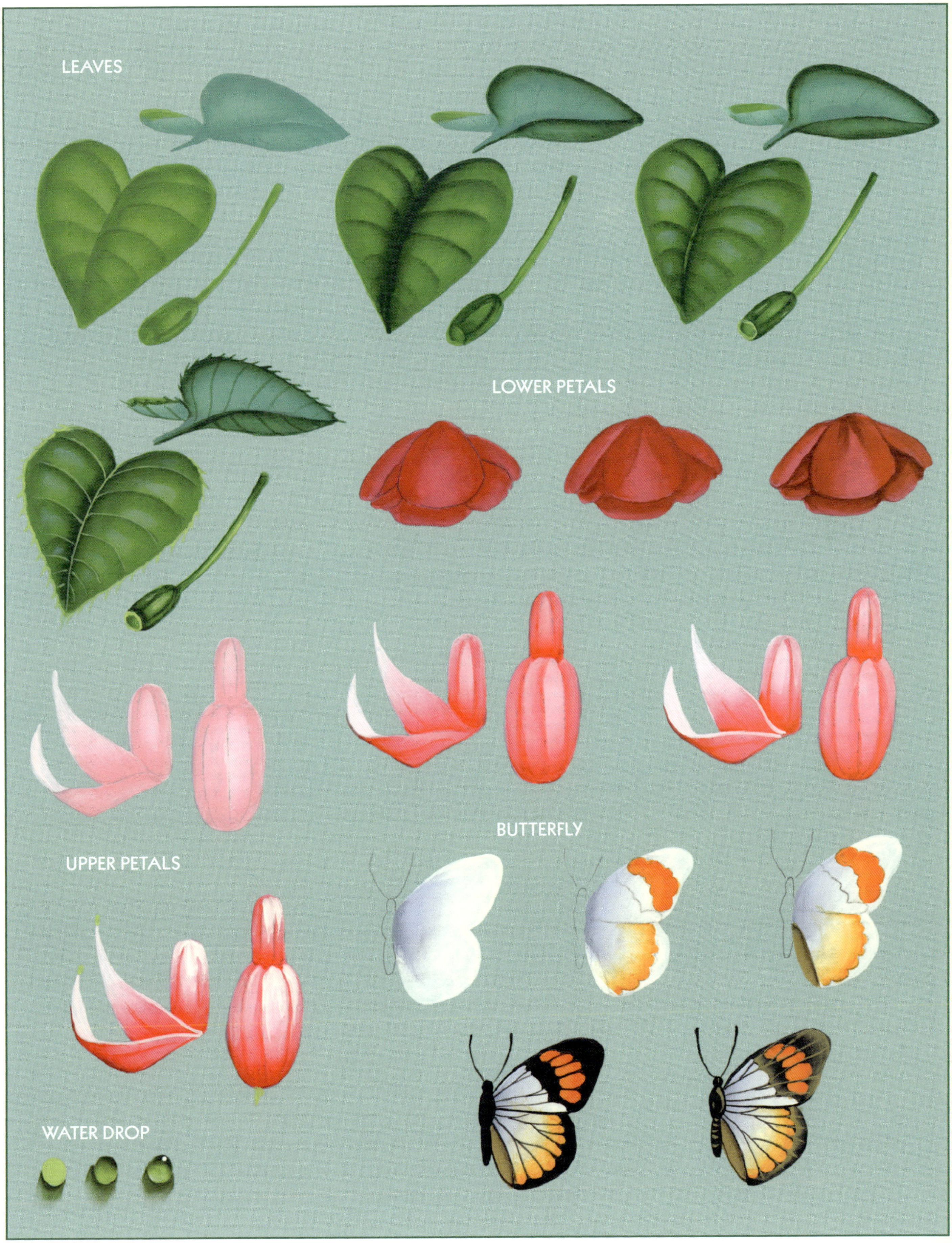
LEAVES
LOWER PETALS
UPPER PETALS
BUTTERFLY
WATER DROP

Fig Basket

Fig leaves and their enticing fruit have inspired artists throughout history. Add a little of their exotic nature to your table with this tray.

MATERIALS

PALETTE

Delta Ceramcoat Acrylics

Black
Blue Haze
Bungalow Blue
Burnt Umber
Cactus Green
Calypso Orange
Dark Brown
Lavender Lace
Lemon Grass
Light Foliage Green
Light Ivory
Light Timberline Green
Maple Sugar Tan
Moroccan Red
Moss Green
Orange
Pumpkin
Raw Sienna
Red Iron Oxide
Salem Green
Straw
Tidepool Blue
Timberline Green

BRUSHES

Loew-Cornell, Inc.

1" wash: Series 7550
#2, #6 and #8 filberts: Series 7500
#2 round: Series 7000
#4 and #8 shaders: Series 7300
¼", ⅜", ½" and ¾" angular shaders: Series 7400
#0 and #1 liners: Series 7350

SURFACE

Wicker tray, 10" square (item #WD7205, *Hofcraft)*
See Resources on page 21

OTHER SUPPLIES

Delta Gel Stain Medium
Delta Gel Blending Medium
Jo Sonja's Retarder and Antiquing Medium

PATTERN

Refer to pattern on page 22.

PREPARATION

Please read carefully the "General Instructions" in the front of the book before starting this project.

1. Stain the wicker and the bottom and inside of the tray with Raw Sienna mixed with lots of water. When dry, brush a coat of *Jo Sonja's Retarder and Antiquing Medium*, about 1½" wide, around the inside edges of the tray. Quickly brush Burnt Umber all around the inside edges over the retarder, being careful to keep it off the wicker. Let set a few seconds, then wipe with a soft cloth, leaving it darker close to the wicker. Allow to dry thoroughly and spray with varnish.

2. Transfer the square to the inside of the tray; basecoat with Light Ivory. Shade around the edges with Maple Sugar Tan, then spatter, also with Maple Sugar Tan, using an old toothbrush. Quickly wipe off any spots that fall on the stained area.

3. Paint a ¼" border around the Light Ivory Square with Lavender Lace, then paint a thin line around the inside and outside of the border, with Tidepool Blue. Paint a diagonal line through each corner of the border, also with Tidepool Blue.

4. Transfer the basic design shapes to the square. Don't transfer the lines for the shadows. These are for reference only.

5. Referring to the pattern, paint the shadows around the drawn shapes, using the following colors: Maple Sugar Tan on the Light Ivory areas; Tidepool Blue on the border areas; Bungalow Blue on the lines around the border; Raw Sienna on the stained areas outside the square.

MAIN (DARK) BRANCH

1. Basecoat with Light Timberline Green.

2. With Timberline Green, shade down both sides, around the cut on the bottom, around the stems, and above the segment lines (see worksheet on page 30).

3. Deepen the shading on the left side and around the cut with Dark Brown; deepen the shading around the stems, above the stem segments and just a little bit below. Leave a small, lighter line at the top of the segments.

4. Re-paint the inside of the cut bottom with Light Timberline Green. Add a Light Timberline Green highlight to the right center and top of the segments.

LEAVES

1. Basecoat the front of the leaves with Cactus Green and the backs with Moss Green. On the front of the leaves, shade around the outside edges and on any areas that are overlapped, using Blue Haze.

2. On the front of the leaves, deepen the shading on the left side and bottom and any overlapped areas, using Salem Green. Shade the back of the center and right hand leaves at the fold and completely around the back of the leaf on the right, using Cactus Green.

3. Paint the main veins with Lemon Grass,

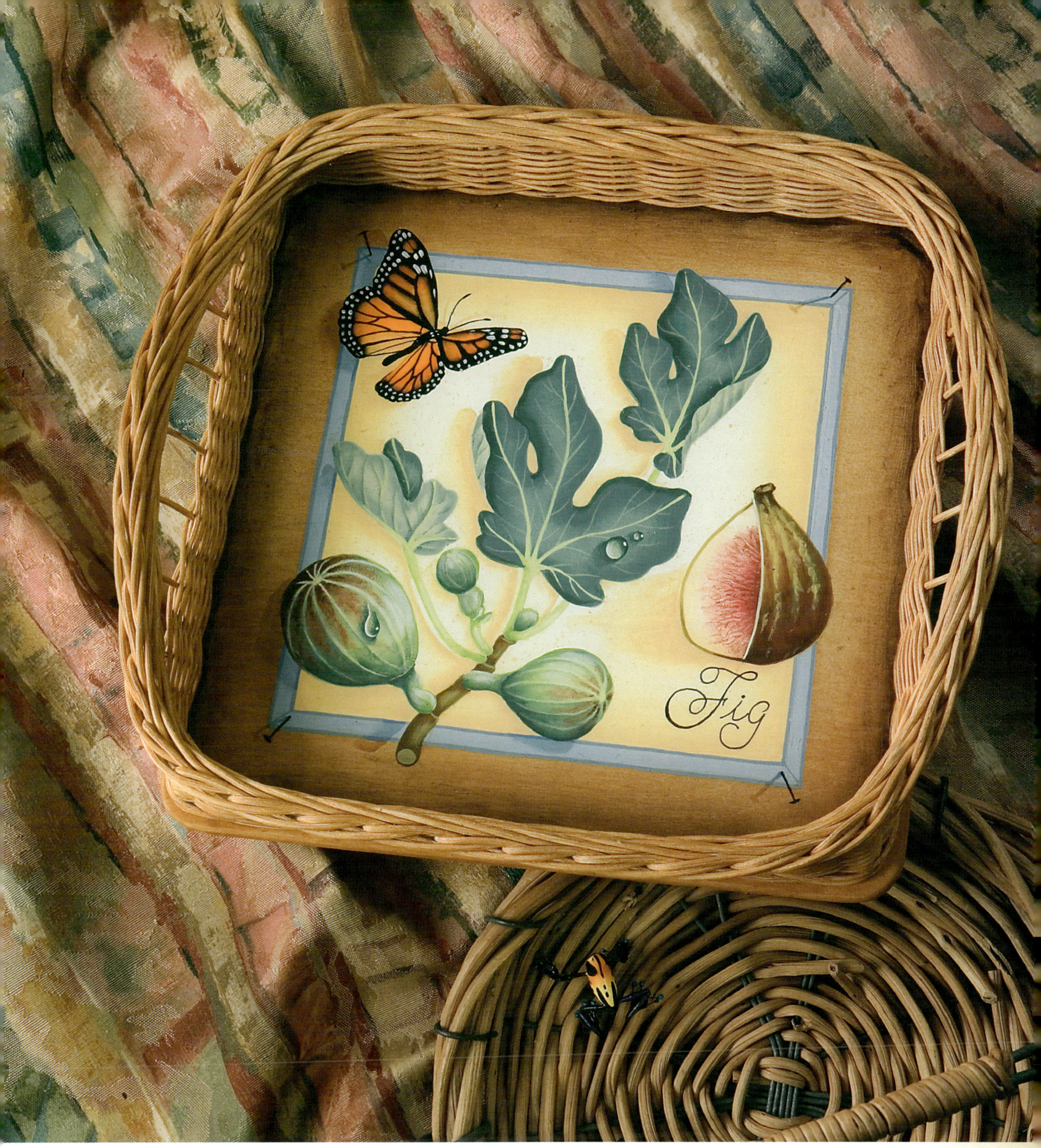

continuing down the stems to where they grow out of the main stem. Add some water to the Lemon Grass to thin, then paint the small side veins. On the back of the leaves, paint a light, thin line with Blue Haze on the left side of the veins.

WATER DROPS ON LEAF

1. Shade around the bottom and partway up the left side of the drop shape with Blue

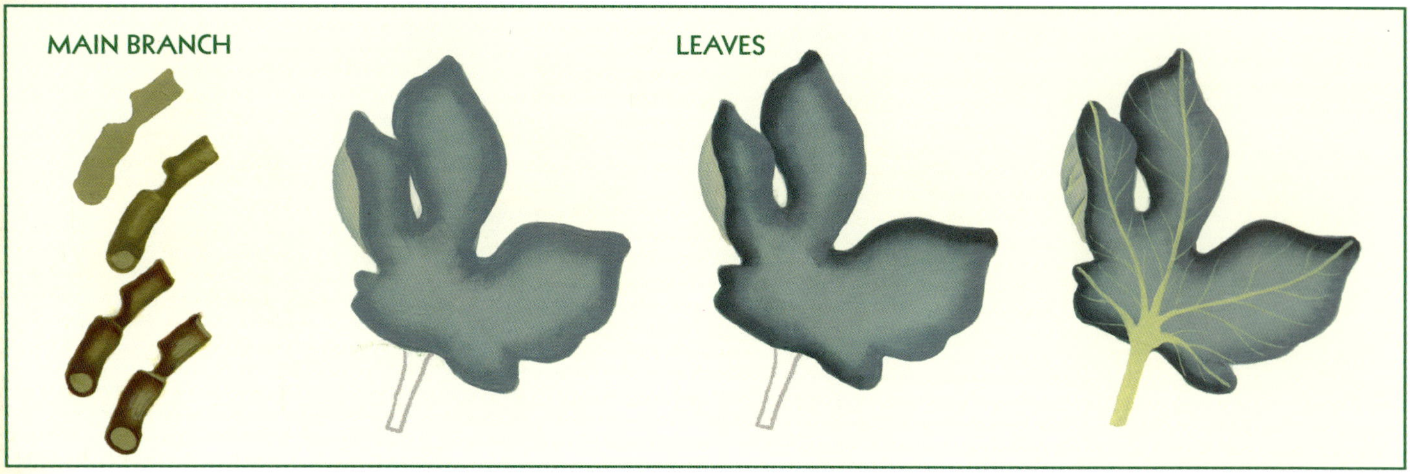

Haze, and deepen with Salem Green. Paint the drop with Lemon Grass, then glaze with a thinned coat of Cactus Green.

2. Shade the drop on the top right with Blue Haze, deepened at the top with Salem Green.

3. Highlight the bottom and partway up the left side with Light Ivory, then dot with Light Ivory in the darkest area of the top right, using the small tip of the stylus.

FIGS ON MAIN BRANCH AND SMALL STEMS

1. Basecoat the figs and remaining small stem with Lemon Grass. Shade all stems, including stems for leaves, on the left side and where they grow out of the main branch, with Light Foliage Green. Shade all around the figs with Light Foliage Green (heavier around the left and bottom).

2. Glaze the figs with a mix of Gel Stain Medium + Cactus Green (1:1). Allow to dry.

3. Add a second glaze around the left and bottom, over the previous shading, with a mix of Gel Stain Medium + Blue Haze (1:1). When dry, deepen this shading with Salem Green.

4. Mix a little Lemon Grass with water and paint the small spot at the large end of the figs, then paint light lines radiating out from this spot, ending at the stem end of the figs. With the Blue Haze Glaze, shade very thinly down the left or lower side of these lines.

5. With a dry #2 filbert brush, pat a little Red Iron Oxide on the large end of the two largest figs between the lines, then deepen at the top by patting on a small amount of Burnt Umber. Touch up the Lemon Grass lines where needed.

6. Highlight the figs with Light Ivory.

WATER DROP ON FIG

1. Shade around the bottom and left side of the drop shape with Blue Haze, and deepen just below the drop with Salem Green. Paint the drop with Lemon Grass, blending it into the fig at the top.

2. Shade the right side with Blue Haze, deepened with Salem Green.

3. Highlight the left side with Light Ivory and dot with Light Ivory on the right side.

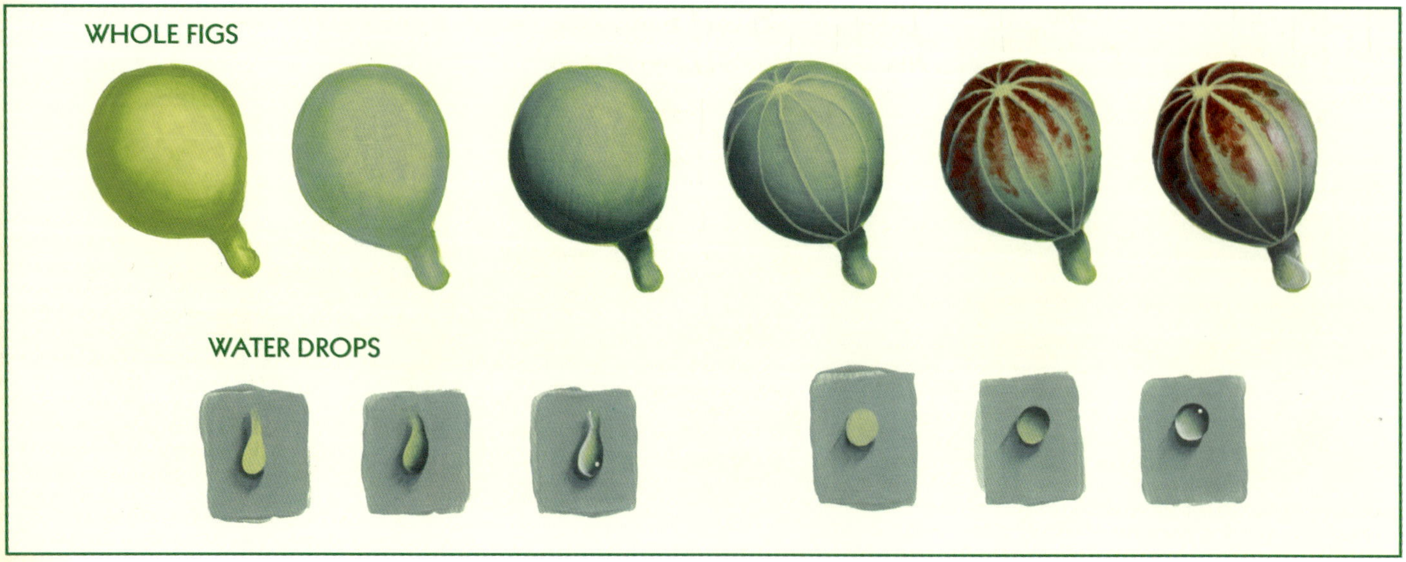

SINGLE CUT FIG

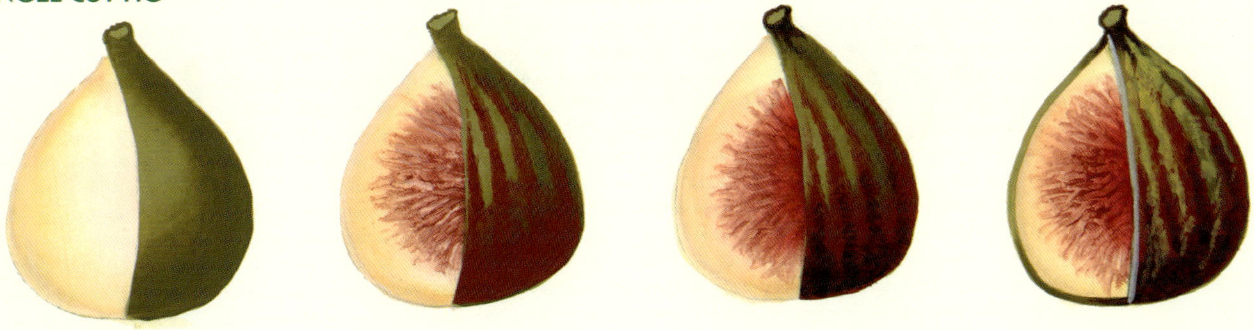

LARGE SINGLE CUT FIG

Note: Paint inside fig first. When thoroughly dry, you might want to carefully tape it off before painting the outside.

Inside

1. Basecoat with Light Ivory, then shade around the outside edge with Maple Sugar Tan.

2. Shade in a half circle next to the cut as follows: Dip the ¾" angular shader in Gel Blending Medium and work through the brush by stroking on the palette. Pick up some Red Iron Oxide, stroke to blend, and float the color on (see worksheet). While this is wet, using a small, dry brush, pull wiggly lines through the Red Iron Oxide from the center toward the outside edges, wiping the paint from the brush frequently. Allow to dry thoroughly.

3. Shade lightly at the center, close to the cut line, with Moroccan Red.

4. Paint a thin line around the outside edge with a mix of Straw + Light Timberline Green (1:1), then shade at the top, along the bottom, and partway up the left side with Timberline Green.

Outside

1. Basecoat the outside of the fig with the Straw/Light Timberline Green mix. Shade around the bottom, almost to the center, around the outside, and around the top with Timberline Green.

2. Deepen the shading on the bottom with Red Iron Oxide, patting some toward the top in stripes, following the contour of the fig.

3. Pat on additional shading with Burnt Umber, at the very bottom of the fig and a short way up the stripes. Darken around the top of the fig and a little across the bottom line around the inside of the fig, using Burnt Umber.

4. Paint a thin Light Ivory line along the cut edge, then highlight the fig between stripes by patting on a little Straw.

BUTTERFLY

1. Base orange areas with Calypso Orange.

2. Shade with Pumpkin around the outside edges of the Calypso Orange on the upper wings and below the upper wing line on the lower wings. Leave the area closest to the body light on the lower left wing.

3. Deepen the shading on the outside edges with Orange.

4. Paint the body, antennae, and black areas and the veins on the wings with Black. Add a very thin Black shading around all Orange areas on the top wings and between the Black edge and Orange area on the lower wings to soften.

5. Add the white accents to the wings and body with Light Ivory.

FINISHING

1. Write the word "Fig" and draw the pins with the black permanent ink fine-line pen.

2. Erase any remaining transfer lines and spray the tray with a couple of coats of satin varnish.

BUTTERFLY

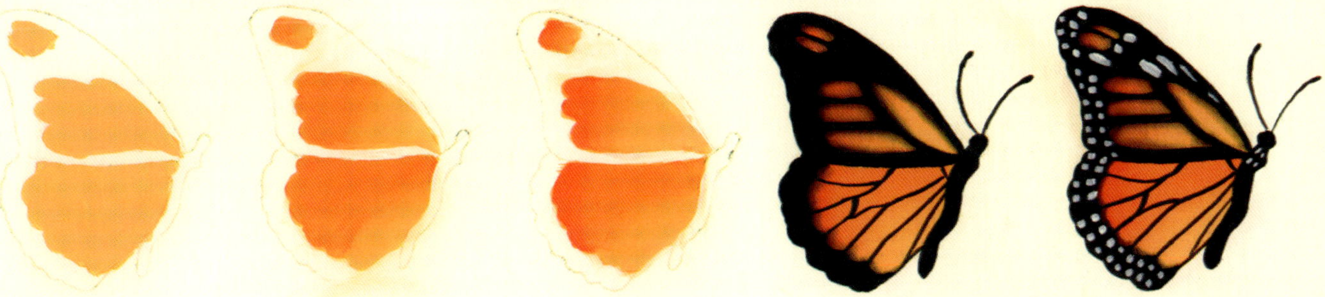

Orange Tray

Bright, fresh, and zesty, this orange tray is perfect for serving afternoon treats to guests and special friends.

MATERIALS

PALETTE

Delta Ceramcoat Acrylics

- Apple Green
- Black
- Blue Lagoon
- Calypso Orange
- Chambray Blue
- Dark Foliage Green
- Lemon Grass
- Light Foliage Green
- Light Ivory
- Light Timberline Green
- Lilac Dusk
- Medium Foliage Green
- Periwinkle Blue
- Pumpkin
- Spice Tan
- Tangerine
- Terra Cotta
- Tidepool Blue
- Timberline Green
- White
- Yellow

BRUSHES

Loew-Cornell, Inc.

1" and 2" wash: Series 7550

#2, #6 and #10 shaders: Series 7300

3/8", 1/2" and 3/4" angular shaders: Series 7400

#6 and #8 filberts: Series 7500

#0 and #2 liners: Series 7350

SURFACE

Round tray, 14" primed metal (item #WT2114, *Hofcraft*)

See Resources on page 21

OTHER SUPPLIES

Delta Metal Primer

Jo Sonja's Retarder and Antiquing Medium

PATTERN

Refer to the center insert.

PREPARATION

Please read carefully the "General Instructions" in the front of the book before starting this project.

1. Since the tray used for this project is pre-primed, no additional metal priming is necessary. Basecoat the inside, including the inside rim, with Light Ivory. Shade around the top of the inside rim with Spice Tan, then spatter the entire inside of the tray with Spice Tan, using an old toothbrush.

2. Basecoat the outside of the tray with Spice Tan. Allow to dry.

3. Spray the inside of the tray with a coat of matte varnish. Dry thoroughly.

4. Transfer the design shapes to the tray.

5. Paint the line around the inside of the tray with Spice Tan.

STEMS, SEPALS, AND SMALL GREEN ORANGE

1. Basecoat with Light Foliage Green. Shade around the cut edges and down the left side of the main stem with Medium Foliage Green.

2. Deepen the shading with Dark Foliage Green. In addition, shade around the sepals and small green orange and wherever a stem grows out from another stem with Dark Foliage Green.

3. Highlight the main stem with Apple Green and paint the cut stem ends with Apple Green. Add a small stroke of Dark Foliage Green to the center of the cut ends (see worksheet on page 34). Highlight the sepals and small green orange with Apple Green.

LEAVES

Front

1. Basecoat with Light Foliage Green.

2. Shade around the outside edges and down both sides of the center vein line with Medium Foliage Green. Add shading where the back overlaps the front of the righthand leaf.

3. Deepen the shading around the outside edges of the leaves, where the back overlaps, and down the left side of the center vein line with Dark Foliage Green.

4. Paint vein lines with Lemon Grass.

5. Highlight between the side vein lines with Apple Green.

Back

1. Basecoat with Light Timberline Green.

2. Shade with Timberline Green.

3. Paint the vein lines with Lemon Grass.

4. Highlight with Lemon Grass.

BLOSSOMS

1. Basecoat with Chambray Blue.

2. Shade with Tidepool Blue (see worksheet).

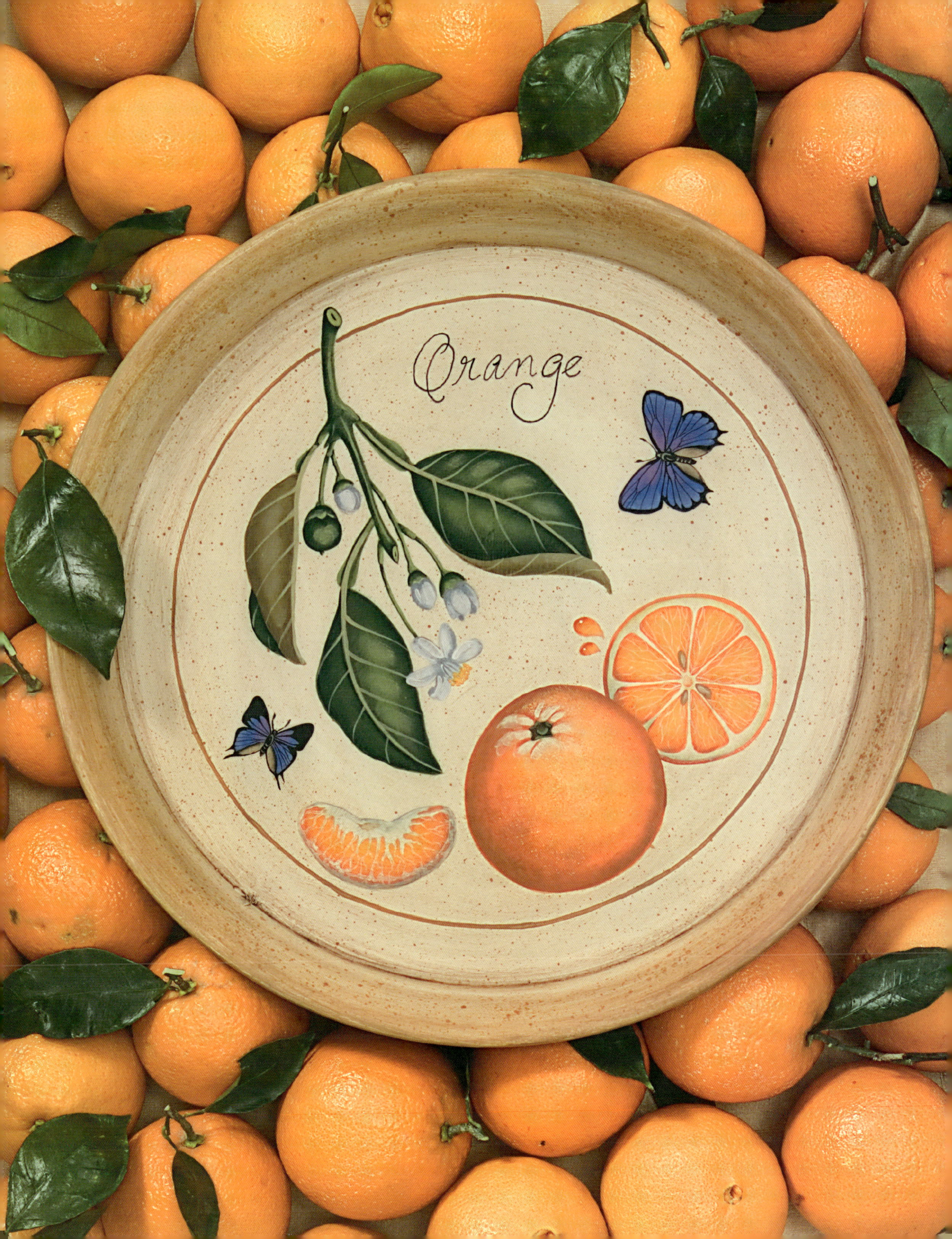
Orange

3. Highlight with White.

4. Dot the ends of the stamens on the open blossom, using the medium stylus tip and Yellow.

ORANGE SLICE

1. Basecoat with White, then paint the segments with Calypso Orange. Paint a Calypso Orange line for the rind just inside the White rim. Glaze the segments with Yellow, then lightly glaze over the outside rind, pith, and center of the slice (over the White) with Yellow.

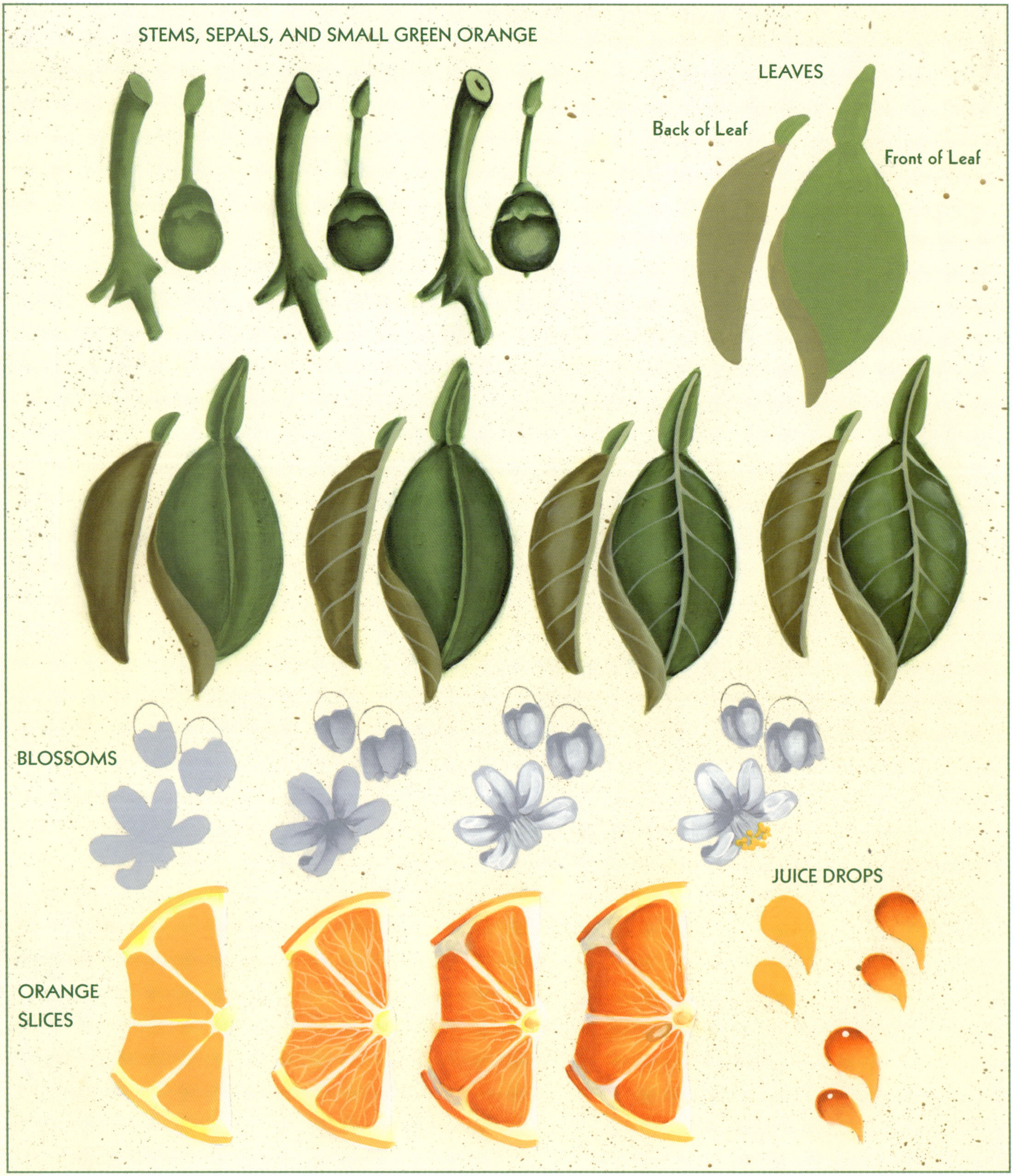

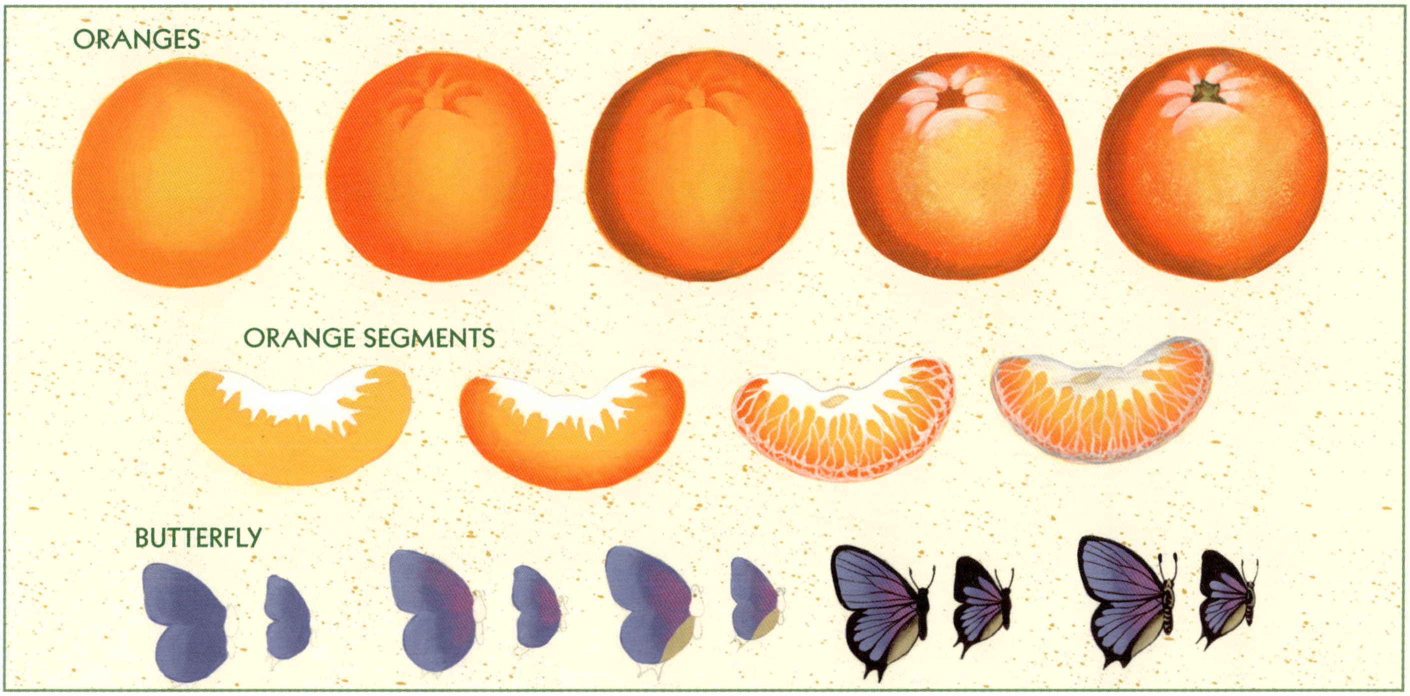

2. Shade around the inside of each segment with Pumpkin. At the same time, using Pumpkin, shade partway around the rind where it appears behind the whole orange. Add the thin White lines to the segments.
3. Shade the rind and segments closest to the whole orange with Terra Cotta, and add a small shading of Terra Cotta to the center. Shade the White in the same area with a light glaze of Chambray Blue.
4. Paint the seeds with Spice Tan, and highlight with Light Ivory.

JUICE DROPS

1. Basecoat with Calypso Orange; glaze with Yellow.
2. Shade around the top of the drops with Pumpkin, then deepen with Terra Cotta.
3. Add a small White highlight dot with the tip of the stylus.

WHOLE ORANGE

1. Basecoat the orange with Calypso Orange, then glaze with Yellow. Shade with Pumpkin, heavier on the left side and bottom of the orange.
2. Deepen the shading with Tangerine. Add the crease lines around the small dried sepal with Tangerine.
3. Further deepen the shading with Terra Cotta.
4. With a sponge, dab on a mix of Yellow + White at the right of center to highlight. Add White highlights between the crease lines (see worksheet). Paint the sepal with Terra Cotta.
5. Shade the sepal with Dark Foliage Green and highlight with Light Foliage Green.

ORANGE SEGMENT

1. Basecoat with White. Paint the orange area with Calypso Orange, then add a Yellow glaze over the Calypso Orange.
2. Shade around the sides and bottom with Pumpkin, followed by Tangerine.
3. Paint the fine White lines (see worksheet). Paint the seed with a mix of Spice Tan + White (1:1).
4. Shade with a glaze of Tidepool Blue; apply a little heavier around the bottom of the segment.

BUTTERFLIES

1. Basecoat the wings with Blue Lagoon, then highlight around the outside wing edges with Periwinkle Blue.
2. Float some Lilac Dusk over the area of the wings closest to the body to highlight.
3. With a mix of Spice Tan + White (1:1), paint the inside segment of the lower wings closest to the body.
4. Paint the body Black and add Black details to the wings. Shade the Spice Tan and White part of the lower wings with Black to soften. Paint a thin Black line around the outside edge of this section.
5. Highlight the body with the Spice Tan/White mix.

FINISHING

1. With the black permanent ink fine-line pen, trace over the "Orange" lettering.
2. Erase any remaining transfer lines.
3. Antique by brushing a coat of *Jo Sonja's Retarder and Antiquing Medium* over the inside of the tray and, while wet, brush on a coat of Burnt Umber. Wait a minute, then wipe off with a clean, soft cloth.
4. Dry thoroughly, then spray with several coats of satin varnish.

Magnolia Box

Combine fragile parchment with a delicately crackled background as you paint this magnificent magnolia blossom with an old-world elegance.

MATERIALS

PALETTE

Delta Ceramcoat Acrylics

AC Flesh
Apple Green
Caribbean Blue
Dark Brown
Dark Foliage Green
Dark Victorian Teal
Dunes Beige
Lemon Grass
Light Foliage Green
Light Ivory
Light Timberline Green
Magnolia White
Medium Foliage Green
Medium Victorian Teal
Mello Yellow
Palomino Tan
Raw Sienna
Rouge
Salem Blue
Timberline Green
Tomato Spice

BRUSHES

Loew-Cornell, Inc.

1" wash: Series 7550
#8 and #10 shaders: Series 7300
⅜", ½" and ¾" angular shaders: Series 7400
#4, #6 and #8 filberts: Series 7500
#1 liner: Series 7350
#2 and #4 rounds: Series 7000

SURFACE

Square cornice box, 12¾" x 3⅛" x 12¾" (item #24571, *Walnut Hollow*)
See Resources on page 21

OTHER SUPPLIES

Delta Fine Crackle Finish, Steps 1 and 2
Delta Antiquing Gel, Black

PATTERN

Refer to the center insert.

PREPARATION

Please read carefully the "General Instructions" in the front of the book before starting this project.

1. Paint the sides of the box with Salem Blue, then shade around the top and bottom edges, on all sides, with Medium Victorian Teal.

2. Cut a 1" square from a sponge and, starting in the middle of one side, stamp a diamond shape around all sides just below the lid opening with Palomino Tan. When this is dry, cut a ½" sponge square and stamp a small diamond between each large diamond, using AC Flesh (see photo on page 38).

3. Paint the top of the box with Salem Blue. Let dry. Transfer the pattern for the parchment paper.

4. Base the parchment with AC Flesh. Shade just inside the edges of the parchment with Palomino Tan. Shade along the fold on the turned-up corners. Spatter, using an old toothbrush and Palomino Tan.

5. Paint around the parchment with Medium Victorian Teal, then shade around the top and right side with Dark Victorian Teal to add the shadow. Paint the hole in the parchment at the top right with Medium Victorian Teal and shade with Dark Victorian Teal. Paint a very thin Dark Victorian Teal line around the bottom and left side of the parchment.

6. Highlight the turned-up corners with Light Ivory, then paint a thin Light Ivory line around the inside edge of the parchment on the top and right side, as well as around the inside edge of the hole in the parchment.

LEAVES

Front

1. Basecoat the front of the leaves with Light Foliage Green. With Medium Foliage Green, shade around the edges, down both sides of the center vein, and above each small side vein (see worksheet on page 39).

2. Deepen the shading around the edges and the right side only of the center vein with Dark Foliage Green. Deepen the shading just above the small side veins.

3. Highlight just below the side vein lines with Caribbean Blue, heavier on the left side.

4. Paint the thin side vein lines and the center vein and stem with Apple Green.

5. Shade up from the bottom of the stem with Raw Sienna, then deepen around the cut edge and partially up the sides with Dark Brown.

Back

1. Basecoat the back of the leaf with Light Timberline Green and shade with Timberline Green.

2. Paint the veins with Lemon Grass, then go over the back with a very light glaze of Raw Sienna.

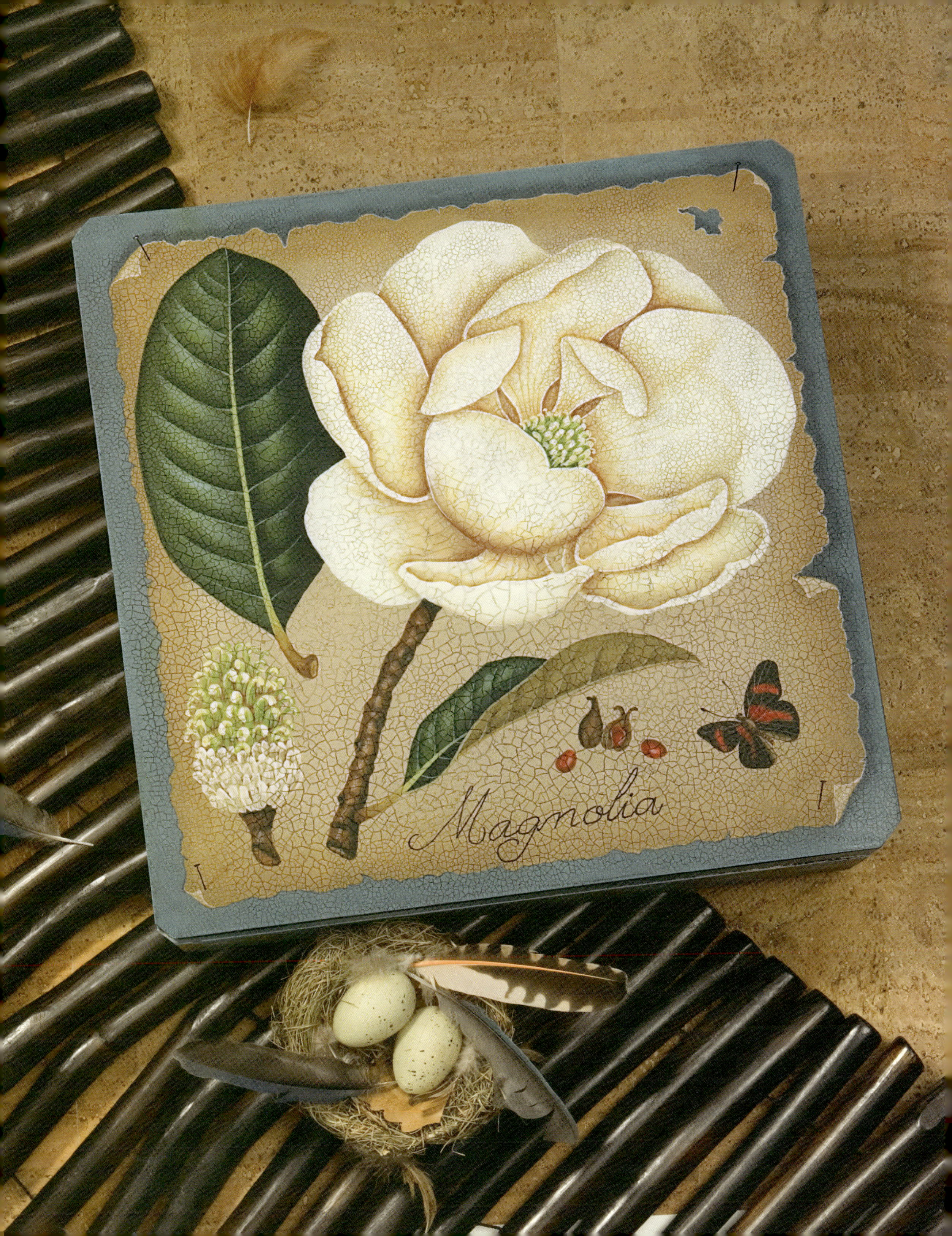
Magnolia

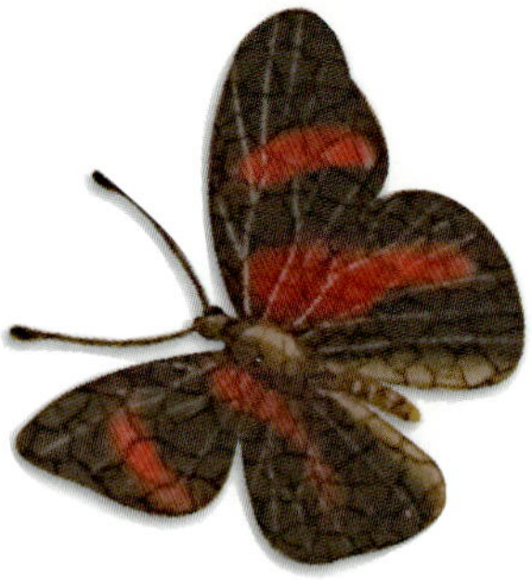

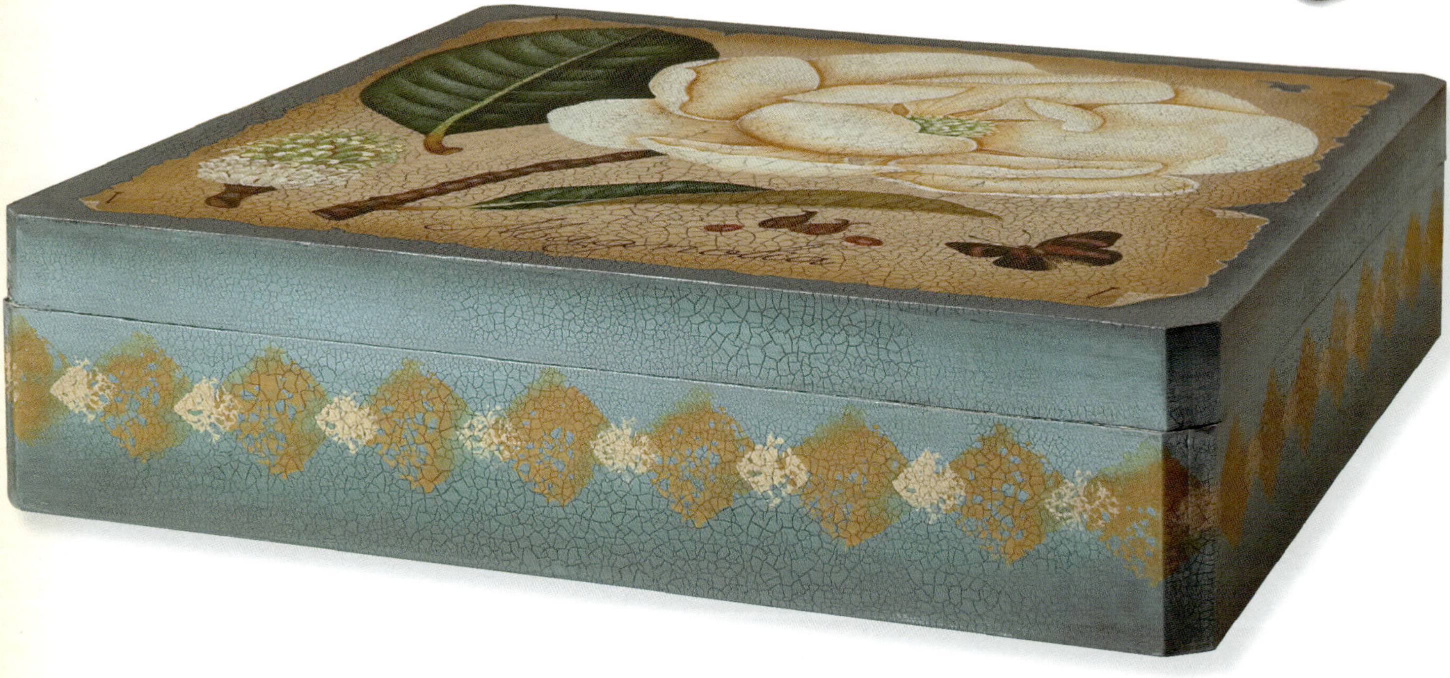

STEMS

1. Paint the stems with Raw Sienna.
2. Shade around the top, above the cut on the bottom, and both sides with Dark Brown. Also shade along the segment lines (see worksheet).
3. Deepen the shading along the top, bottom, and right sides with Dark Foliage Green. Add some leaf nodules with Dark Foliage Green.
4. Highlight with Lemon Grass.

MAGNOLIA FRUIT

(Just under large leaf)

1. Basecoat the shape with Palomino Tan and glaze with Dark Brown.
2. Over this, on the top section, paint the stamens with Light Foliage Green in a curved-top cane shape (see worksheet).
3. Paint the anthers (curved tops) and part way down the sides of the stamens with Apple Green.
4. Highlight the anthers with Mello Yellow, then paint some of the anthers in the center with Magnolia White.
5. For the bottom section, dip a #4 round brush in Palomino Tan, tip with Light Ivory and, starting at the top, make downward strokes, curving toward the stem. Highlight with Magnolia White.

BUTTERFLY

1. Basecoat the wings with Rouge, then shade close to the body with Tomato Spice. Paint the section of the lower wings closest to the body with Palomino Tan.
2. Paint the dark areas of wings with a mix of Dark Brown + Dark Foliage Green (2:1).
3. Shade around Rouge and Palomino Tan edges with the same mix to soften (see worksheet). Paint a very thin line around outside of the Palomino Tan section with the mix. Paint body with Raw Sienna and shade on the left side and around the head and middle of the body with the Dark Brown + Dark Foliage Green mix. Paint the eyes and antennae with the same mix.
4. Highlight the body with Palomino Tan. Add the wing veins with Palomino Tan.

MAGNOLIA BLOSSOM

1. Basecoat with Light Ivory. Referring to photo for placement, shade with AC Flesh (see worksheet, page 40), and shade around the base of each petal and wherever one petal overlaps another.
2. Deepen the shading with Dunes Beige, then just a small amount of Raw Sienna. Paint very fine lines, out from the base of each petal, with Raw Sienna.
3. Highlight with Magnolia White.

Flower Center

1. Basecoat the center with Light Foliage Green, then shade all around with Medium Foliage Green.

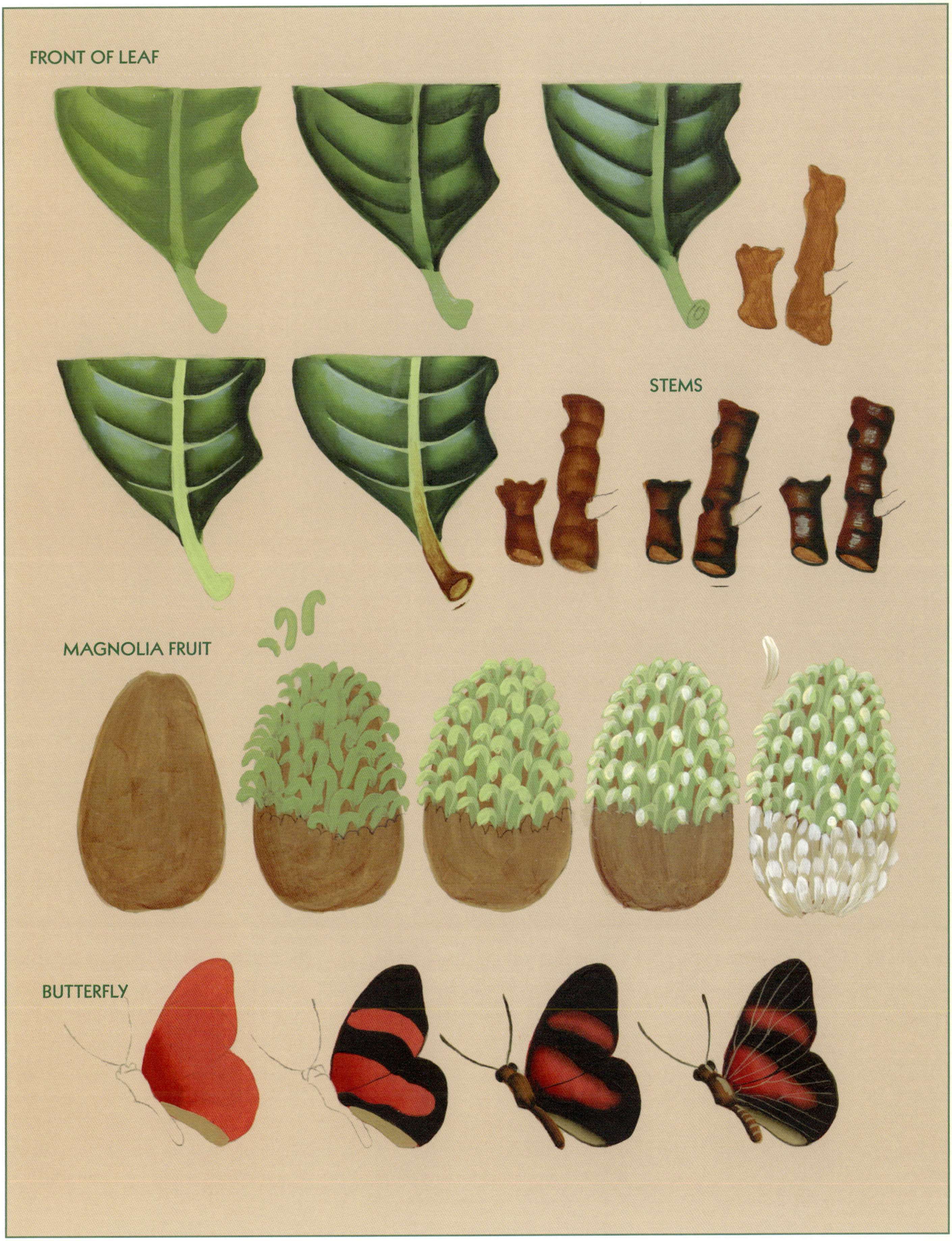
FRONT OF LEAF
STEMS
MAGNOLIA FRUIT
BUTTERFLY

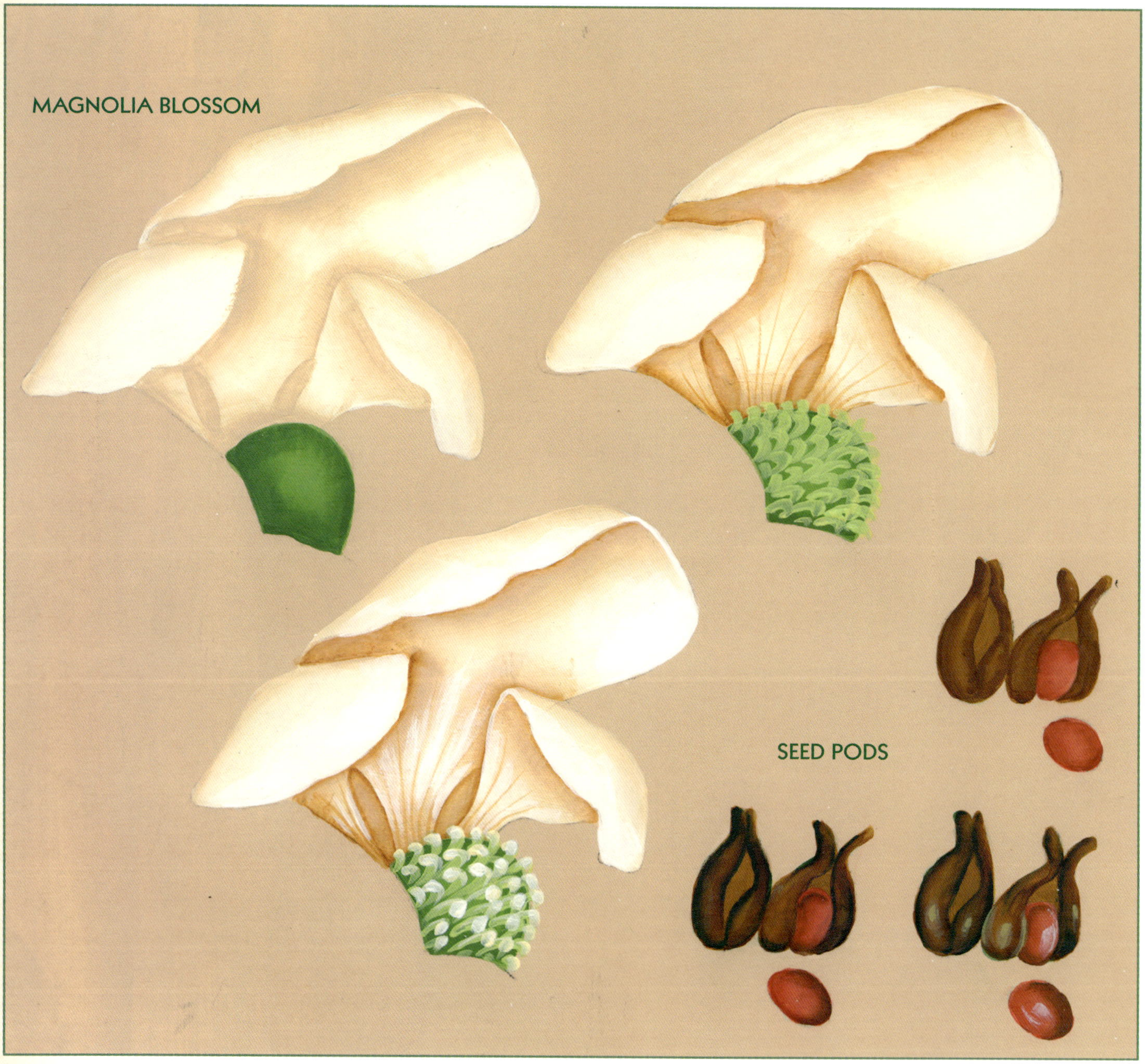

2. Paint the stamens with Apple Green.

3. Paint the anthers with Mello Yellow, then highlight the center anthers with Magnolia White.

SEED PODS

1. Basecoat with Raw Sienna; shade with Dark Brown.

2. Deepen the shading with Dark Foliage Green.

3. Highlight with Palomino Tan.

SEEDS

1. Paint the seeds with Rouge, then shade all around with Tomato Spice.

2. Deepen the shading with Dark Brown.

3. Highlight with Light Ivory.

FINISHING

1. With the black permanent ink fine-line pen, trace over the word "Magnolia"

2. Erase any remaining transfer lines.

3. Following the directions on the bottles carefully, brush on Step 1 of the *Delta Fine Crackle Finish* (keeping in mind that the thicker Step 1 is brushed on, the larger the cracks. Varying the thickness of Step 1 gives a more realistic and interesting look). When dry, brush on Step 2. Dry overnight.

4. Brush on some *Delta Antiquing Gel, Black* and immediately wipe off. Apply lightly or it'll look too harsh. If you don't feel you have used enough, let dry and repeat.

5. Spray with satin varnish.